Availabi

Availability . . .

The Problem and the Gift

Robert J. Wicks

Paulist Press • New York • Mahwah

Library of Congress
Catalog Card Number: 85-62868

ISBN: 0-8091-2767-9

Published by Paulist Press
997 Macarthur Boulevard
Mahwah, N.J. 07430

Printed and bound in the United States of America

Contents

Acknowledgments

My work owes a special debt to the pioneering efforts of Henri Nouwen. His integrated work on relationships—with self, others, and God—is contained in all his books, especially in his classic work *Reaching Out* and in his simple clearly written book on desert spirituality and contemporary ministry, *The Way of the Heart*. If anything, I hope *Availability* reflects in some small way the positive spirit of his beautiful efforts. In a similar way I would like to acknowledge the influence Thomas Merton and Anthony Bloom have had on my work. Both men saw "prayer" and "life" as two different words for the same thing. Their vision of unity in approaching God made self-awareness, compassion with others, and contemplation different turns on the same road to finding and living the Truth.

Support for my work also comes in different ways from a number of other sources. Probably the greatest impact on the final form this book takes does not come from anyone quoted or listed in a bibliographic entry. Yet, this "invisible influence" is present on almost every page. Her ideas, editorial suggestions, and spirituality made *Availability* become a real possibility. And so, to my wife Michaele, I express my love and appreciation. Hopefully, I have somehow in this book brought to life the beauty and insights she shared and continues to share with me.

There have also been other people who contributed to my efforts. Father Kevin Lynch of Paulist Press believed in the idea from its inception; Sister Christa Marie Thompson, O.S.F. reviewed the manuscript for style and format; Barbara Price and Nancy Kosmowsky typed draft after draft of the work; *Review for Religious* gave me permission to adapt "Failure and Forgiveness in Ministry" for use as a chapter in this book; and finally, my daughter Michaele and my friends Rick and Karen Parsons each gave me a special personal gift which kept me full of energy during the project—they were *available* to me when I needed someone to be at my side, and for this I can't thank them enough.

Dedication

In memory of Sister Marie Antoine, I.H.M., I would like to dedicate this book to the Sister Servants of the Immaculate Heart of Mary. She so loved her congregation and I think I know the reason; because when I am with them, I too can experience the Lord's gentle healing presence. May they continue to be truly available to themselves, others . . . and *God*.

Availability:
A Brief Introduction

Availability is a simple but great gift. The freedom to be present when needed is something special. It is an opportunity to be *spiritual*—to be open to relationship in the deepest, most elegant sense of the term. Yet, this wonderful state of living often seems hidden or distorted now. Today, availability is at a premium.

Some of us are "too available." Thus, true availability becomes watered down. We become too busy to pray, too tired to reflect, and, ironically, too stimulated interpersonally to really be *present* to others.

Others among us pull back in anxiety. Being available to God seems to raise too many questions or doubts. Spending time alone is no longer relaxing; instead we feel lonely or preoccupied with our faults and failures. And being with others doesn't seem to help either; in some cases, we feel used, left out, or misunderstood. The end result is that our expectations for intimacy are not realized and we feel the need to pull back more than ever.

This situation is not merely a sad one; it is *dangerous*. Without a sense of availability to self, others and God, life loses its spirituality. Relationships suffer, break down, and we are left with a void or sense of confusion.

We must address availability with the imperative that openness to the personal and interpersonal is essential if the Spirit is to be heard . . . *felt*. Any blocks to relationship must be removed if we are to prepare ourselves always for the continual coming of what is Good. The very vitality of living out

1

the Gospel depends on our being involved—in an ongoing way—in this process.

Recently when I was in Ireland, I became lost while traveling the back roads near the small west coast town of Corafinne. When I stopped alongside the road to ask directions of a gentleman working there, the brief stop turned into a lovely fifteen minute encounter. I not only received directions but I also found that we wound up talking about a myriad of things.

As I drove away, I thought, "Wasn't it nice that he took out time to talk to me." As I drove a bit farther it finally dawned on me what really had occurred. He hadn't taken out time from his day to be with me; *he had made me part of his life*.

This kind of attitude is at the heart of a life that reflects an appreciation of the gift of availability. This story merits being kept in mind as we look at some of the basic problems we encounter in trying to be available to ourselves, others, and God. Though the concept is simple, living a life of true availability isn't simple for most of us.

I

Being Available to . . . Ourselves

Introduction

To be as available as possible to others requires that we be continually aware of who we are psychologically, and where we are spiritually. In other words, we must make an effort to be as "self-aware" as possible.

This point is obviously not a new one. Therapists have long pointed to the need for those wishing to be helpers to be involved in a continuous process of self-examination. In addition, religious figures (e.g., Teresa of Avila) long pre-dated psychologists in emphasizing the same sentiment from a theological vantage point; self-awareness and knowledge of God go hand in hand. Thus, from a psychological perspective we must seek to learn what our unconscious agendas and motivations are, whereas from a religious stance we must always strive to discern where the spirit is leading us.

In light of this need to be appreciative of how the "Christian Self" is developing, four topics are presented in this section on *Being Available to Ourselves:* "uniqueness," "failure and forgiveness," "self-awareness," and "clarity."

They are all in accordance with the following theme: the more we can remove the blocks to an appreciation of who we are and who we are becoming, the truer we can be in our response to the Gospel call to serve others and God. We must be available then to ourselves so that our relationships can flow out of a healthy attitude and a clear awareness of our motivations.

Consequently, the theme of this section is based on the belief that:

> We must understand and preserve ourselves *at all costs* . . . not merely so that we might survive, but also that Christ might live on in us and in those whom we touch in his name.

1

Uniqueness

The Rabbi Zusya said a short time before his death, "In the world to come, I shall not be asked, 'Why were you not Moses?' Instead, I shall be asked, 'Why were you not Zusya?' "

—*Martin Buber*[1]

A significant turning point in therapy or counseling arrives when the individual seeking help is able to grasp the following, simple, seemingly paradoxical reality:

When we truly accept our limits, the opportunity for personal growth and development is almost limitless.

Prior to achieving this insight, energy is wasted on running away from the self, or running to another image of self. We fear being ourselves and lack the necessary trust in God for personal evolution to take place. Therefore, running in confusion we fail to take the special place in community that creation has destined for us.

I guess this is not surprising because we are constantly bombarded with the message that we should be someone or something else. Movies and cartoons impress us with how wonderful it would be if animals and machines could speak, and people could rise above the story of Genesis, successfully eat of the fruit of the tree of knowledge and be supermen, and gods. There is little call for people to fulfill their destiny, and much energy (and money!) is expended on convincing them to avoid it at all costs. In e.e. cummings' words, "To be nobody but yourself in a world which is doing its best, night and day, to make you everybody else—means to fight the hardest battle which any human being can fight, and never stop fighting."

This movement away from the evolution of our true nature flies in the face of our heritage. The courageous people ("saints") who came before us taught us important lessons about "uniqueness." In their struggles they offered us models of the need to strive with all our might to be ourselves. In the words of the famous inventor and global citizen, R. Buckminster Fuller:

> The only important thing about me is that I am an average, healthy human being. All the things I've been able to do, any human being, or any one, or you, could do equally well or better. I was able to accomplish what I did by refusing to be hooked on a game of life that had nothing to do with the way the universe was going. I was just a throwaway who was willing to commit myself to what needed to be done.

As Christians, the philosophy of Fuller is translated into accepting a very essential point of faith: the same Spirit given to Jesus is available for us to receive; and in living in the Spirit we seek not another world for ourselves but the evolution of the kingdom of God in ourselves and the world community. This, rather than a life of denial and fantasy, is the very thrill and challenge of life.

Einstein said, "He who can no longer pause to wonder and stand rapt in awe is as good as dead." This point is valid to no greater degree than in appreciating the loveliness of our uniqueness when we respond to the Spirit that is calling us to *be*.

A woman who had a miscarriage in the final trimester of her pregnancy taught me the importance of the uniqueness of every human being. When I asked her how she felt about losing her baby, she indicated that she was naturally quite sad about it, but there was one specific thing that particularly upset her:

> When I think of the son or daughter I lost, the one point which tears me apart the most is that I shall never know who my child was . . . what he or she was like. Would he have been a hyperactive boy? Would she have been a pensive girl? I'll never know, and that is a special sadness for me.

We who do live, who have been born, and who have a personality which can be known by us and shared with others have a duty to let it evolve. If we don't seek to let the Spirit grow within us but instead abort our talents, we mock existence and our singular place in it. In fact, the community (of saints) is significantly lessened by our absence.

To develop fully requires an appreciation of the value each of us has. It also requires to a great degree a recognition of our natural resistance to continue on the path toward truth. In addition, development necessitates an acceptance of the gift of laughter—laughter at the false self which tries to capture our imagination in a way which makes us competitive, driven, and insecure.

Resistance

John Sanford in his book *Healing and Wholeness* echoes a theme, often stressed by Teresa of Avila, that even when we believe in the value of the continuing search for ways to develop, the process can be a discouraging battle. In the words of Sanford,

> Deep inside each organism is something that knows what that organism's true nature and life goal is. It is as though

there is within each person an inner center that knows
what constitutes health. If our conscious personality becomes related to the inner center, the whole person may
begin to emerge, though this may not bring either peace
or social adaptation, but conflict and stress. . . . The
movement toward health may look more like a crucifixion
than adaptation or peace of mind.[2]

The struggle to help the whole person emerge requires a
strong belief in the importance of not turning away from the
Light. The relief gained in putting up our defenses and avoiding the truth is only a temporary one. The trade-off for igno-
rance is too great, for in not fighting the good fight, we die a
bit each day torn by our anxieties and compulsions which keep
us troubled, bored, and unsatisfied.

So, in bringing all our efforts to remove the blocks to our
natural call to grow, we must expect a battle. Realizing the lure
of avoiding self-knowledge, we must seek psychological helps
to aid us in our conversion (*metanoia*) to the Word which calls
us to take our place at the table. One of the key human helps
to this process which should not be overlooked is our ability to
laugh.

Laughter and Perspective

Norman Cousins, who wrote the book *Anatomy of an Illness*
(and was the only layperson to my knowledge ever to have an
article published in the *New England Journal of Medicine*), lauded
the value of laughter. He noted that ten minutes of belly laughter from watching comedic episodes on TV would help him
achieve two hours of pain-free sleep. This result, he said,
proved to him the statement that "laughter is good medicine."
I would like to add to this that *if laughter is in fact good medicine,
then laughing at ourselves and our defenses must surely be healing.*

We have a tendency to take ourselves too seriously in a bad way. In light of this, as humans we often become so attuned to our faults that we fear failing and forget forgiveness. This very process results in our failing to have energy available for self-exploration while we are trying to find Christ in our involvement with others. The cost of such a process is loss of touch with a very basic truth: that before we were born, God's grace was already present to embrace us for a lifetime.

This very point leads us into the subject of the next chapter—namely, the need to inextricably tie failure and forgiveness together in our search for relationship with self, others, and God. Without such an understanding, uniqueness is doomed to be lost in defensive deformity and the possibility for self-awareness is destined to be terribly diminished. Thus, instead of embracing and preserving our uniqueness as a Gift of the Spirit, we let it fall into disuse, whereas, with an appreciation of our special talents, our ministry becomes a source of inspiration for the common good as well as a source of light for determining our own true needs.

Please Note:

A brief biblical quotation capturing a major theme of the preceding material appears at the end of each chapter. For persons wishing to use this book as part of a daily prayer/retreat experience, the following procedure is suggested. Read the chapter, than take a few minutes to reflect on it. After this is done, read the biblical quotation slowly once or twice, then take twenty or thirty minutes in silence and (if possible) solitude to let the quotation nurture you. Don't analyze it; don't think about it. Just be silent and let it become part of you.

†   †   †

1 Corinthians 12:4–11

There are different gifts but the same Spirit; there are different ministries but the same Lord; there are different works but the same God who accomplishes all of them in everyone. To each person the manifestations of the Spirit is given for the common good. To one the Spirit gives wisdom in discourse, to another the power to express knowledge. Through the Spirit one receives faith; by the same Spirit another is given the gift of healing, and still another miraculous powers. Prophecy is given to one; to another, power to distinguish one spirit from another. One receives the gift of tongues, another that of interpreting the tongues. But it is one and the same Spirit who produces all these gifts, distributing them to each as he wills.

2

Failure and Forgiveness

Most laymen, he supposed, believed psychiatrists fell
apart under the weight of other people's problems.
Dr. Theodore Levin had another theory. He feared
that a psychiatrist's life force gradually leaked out. It
was expended on sympathy, understanding, the obsessive need to heal and help create whole lives. Other
people's lives. But always from the outside. Always
the observer.
Then one day he would wake up and discover that he
himself was empty, drained.

—*Lawrence Sanders*[1]

Involved Christians fail a great deal. We probably don't
like to talk about it, but it's true. As a group, we fail as much,
if not *more*, than any other community concerned with helping
others in need. This should not be surprising since with greater
commitment there is a greater "opportunity" to miss at least
some of the numerous goals we set for ourselves in life.

Yet, despite the fact that as Christians we court failure as
a natural part of our idealism, many of us still look upon missing the mark with great disdain and embarrassment. We forget
the lessons we have been taught about the intimate relationship
between commitment and failure. I know; I certainly fit into
this group.

As a small boy and later as a high school and college
youth, I remember not only being asked to reflect on a character such as Winston Churchill in his finest hour, but also to
look at him and others in their moments of personal and profes-

sional defeat. The message was: with any successful commitment comes poignant, frequent failure as well. Unfortunately,
that message doesn't always stick with us.

Instead many of us try to deny and avoid failure at all
costs. We look upon certain Christian "gurus" as invincible,
while in turn we allow others to put us up on pedestals. All of
this seems to go well until our models tarnish and we—in an
effort to be perfect—stumble, fall, and are forced to see a natural fact of life: We have needs. We get tired. We lose fervor.
We fail too!

The best and worst of us experience failure. It can occur
when we're dealing with persons (friends, relatives, colleagues,
anyone who turns to us for help) with overwhelming long-
standing difficulties who have a paucity of resources, or it can
come about when we "over-attend" to those with great potential who are only in need of some temporary support and guidance. With the former we may not push hard enough; with the
latter we may move too directly and, paternalistically, we may
smother their independence by trying to force our "solutions"
upon them. In both instances, those who came to us for help
may turn away, leaving us with a deep sense of doubt about
our roles in life. It takes courage and faith to face ourselves
when we realize we have failed the needy or misled the tal-
ented.

At times like this, we may be prompted to ask ourselves,
"Why am *I* in the role of minister? I'm experiencing many of
the same challenges and doubts that they are. How and why,
then, am I being called upon to help?" Those of us who are in
ministry as counselors, spiritual directors, teachers, religious
educators, or Christian leaders can readily identify with these
personal doubts. When we stand back and survey the kind of
people who come to us for guidance, we recognize that some
are brighter, some more attractive, some healthier, and many
holier! The question then is, "Where do we fit in? What is it

that marks us in a specific instance as the minister?" In attempting to answer this question, we as Christians must grapple with several factors that may distinguish us from those who seek our help.

Three such factors which make us different from (not better than) the persons to whom we are ministering are:

1. A body of knowledge (e.g., religion, psychology, theology, spirituality) or experience and an ability to be more objective, which we can draw upon to help others;
2. A recognition that persons come to us for help with *specific* needs at *certain* junctures in their lives. They do this so we may be an instrument to help them gain the light, not because we *are* the light. They do not come because our lives are so successful; they usually come because their own lives seem presently confused or full of failure;
3. A psychological and theological appreciation of forgiveness which allows us to learn from our own failures instead of being crushed by them; in psychological jargon, we model self-acceptance. Or, from a popular theological perspective, we recognize (as aptly noted on a bumper sticker seen at a seminary) that "Christians aren't perfect . . . they're forgiven."

It is this third point—having a sense of perspective regarding failure and forgiveness—that might well be the most crucial of the three and is the one which we shall look at in more depth here.

Psychology of "Burnout", Theology of Hope

As was noted earlier, direct reference to failure among Christian leaders has frequently been avoided. However, recent timely writings on the psychology of "burnout"[2] and the theology of hope[3] have helped us to put our unsuccessful attempts at ministry in their proper place.

The literature on burnout points out clearly something most of us already had an inkling about: namely, undisciplined activism may lead to a depletion of personal resources. The emotional well can and will run dry if we don't take preventive actions. In this light, true self-ministry based on self-awareness is not a luxury; it is a necessity if we are to avoid unnecessary Christian masochism on the one hand, or withdrawal and privatism on the other.

A sound theology of hope also has shown itself to be an important element in handling daily stress and personal failures, although the help it provides is not tied to a total release from the burden of life. A Christologically-based theology of hope doesn't release us from the pain of the "now" of existence. Ironically, it may even offer us more pain—the pain of knowing we are responsible to and for others, the pain of yearning and groaning for the coming of the kingdom of God (Romans 8:21). Yet, on the other hand, it is helpful to have faith in God's promises. With a theology of hope that has as its *ground* the vindication of God's promises to us in the resurrection of Jesus, that has as its *object* the universality of the scope of redemption, and that has as its *subject* the dualism of this age and the age to come, we can face today's world with some understanding and logic. We can recognize that while we shouldn't stand quietly staring into the heavens (Acts 1:10ff), we also needn't feel that we have the future of the world solely in our own hands.[4]

An appreciation of both the psychology of burnout and a sound theology of hope, then, can lay the groundwork for envisioning our failures in a way that leads to greater knowledge and clarity rather than to proof that our efforts to reach out to others in need are just pure folly. However, to accomplish such a healthy approach to our failures, we also specifically need a balanced view of *forgiveness* which will lead to *self-understanding, knowledge*, and *clarity*.

Forgiveness

To accomplish this we must recognize and avoid false forms of forgiveness. "Pseudo-forgiveness" often parades itself as a form of true self-acceptance. However, by its "fruits" it is possible to discern in ourselves and others whether or not the sense of forgiveness is properly oriented. There are surely numerous forms of pseudo-forgiveness. The one that particularly concerns us here is the one which forgets our humanity, inordinately focuses on the shame of our failures, and leads to an unproductive confession based only on ventilation of our sins.

It occurs when we forget that in trying to be virtuous (in the best sense of the word) we can and *will* eventually fail; we forget that in trying to reach out to others, our own limits and needs must sometimes get in the way. We forget that we can and should learn from our failures, *not* see them as proof that we shouldn't be Christian activists or helpers.

When we as committed Christians lose our perspective with regard to failure, we ignore the need for self-acceptance as a prelude to personal growth. Instead of forgiveness leading to an openness which will in turn translate into self-understanding, it leads to self-punishment. In such a case as this, we believe that we are seeking forgiveness by crucifying ourselves for our weaknesses. As we do this, the energy formerly reserved for knowledge gets destructively channeled off into changing the process of self-understanding into one of self-condemnation. Nothing positive is accomplished when this happens.

Ironically, this hurtful process of repentance *prevents* rather than enhances change and growth. The most obvious reason for this is that we are less apt to look at our behavior objectively if we are embarrassed or pained by reflection on it. Therefore, behavior that we wince at usually eventually turns into behavior that we wink at. If it causes us too much discomfort to look at something, psychologically we will avoid it through repression, suppression, denial, rationalization, and by general distortion of it. Let's face it—who wants to look at something unpleasant . . . unless, of course we are masochistic? This brings us to a second point.

To be saddened by the disappointment others have in us when we don't meet their expectations is part of the necessary pain of Christian service; to depress ourselves for the same set of failures, however, is a futile exercise in Christian masochism. Such a process also drains off the energy necessary for a self-examination which can turn a mistake into an opportunity for increased perceptual clarity. Instead it wastes what motivation we have, puts us on an inappropriate psychological path, and closes the door to the love of God that is always reflected in healthy self-love. Clearly, if Grace is "the one energy that makes life good,"[5] then self-punishment is an unconscious enemy of such positive movements in our lives.

In essence, then, psychological burnout, worshiping despair instead of grasping onto a sound theology of hope, and losing touch with human self-acceptance and real Christian forgiveness can turn failure into a dark, dreaded defeat. Yet the opposite process is not only possible, but it is necessary if we are to remain as undepleted, increasingly-aware servants of others in need.

Even in failure we can learn; even in failure we can be close, very close to God. Failure does not have the power to change that; only our distorted perceptions of failure make us think it can. Keeping this in mind is a major initial step on the road to keeping psychically alive amidst our lost successes in ministry. This is essential to remember because, despite our failures, we need to continue our work. The world craves for the energy of helpers who fail but who can succeed in remembering that they are forgiven and can attempt to model this important Christian reality for others. It is this kind of testimony that makes us *different* . . . it is this kind of attitude that makes it possible even amidst failure to demonstrate a special response to God.

† † †

John 3:16–17

Yes, God so loved the world
that he gave his only Son,
that whoever believes in him may not die
but may have eternal life.
God did not send the Son into the world
to condemn the world,
but that the world might be saved through him.

3

Self-Awareness

It is as hard to see oneself as to look backwards without turning round . . .
                                    —*Henry David Thoreau*[1]

Softly looking at ourselves does not mean glossing over
our difficulties or faults. It means viewing ourselves through
Christ's compassionate eyes so that we can gain the vision to
"go and sin no more" (John 8:11).

Power comes from such true self-awareness. For in really
seeing ourselves, we see the almost unbelievable: we are actually witnesses to God's activity embraced within *our own*
thoughts, feelings, and actions. The primary end of this vision
is not personal peace or security; instead, it is a search designed
to foster the necessary *self love*, *Christian power*, and *courage* essential to "Christian life."

Self-awareness and self-love go hand in hand. Kenneth
Leech states in his book *True Prayer*, "You do not want to know
someone whom you despise, even if, especially if, that someone is you."[2] One feeds the other and forms a positive circle.
Self-esteem is really Christian self-awareness. The more we
seek Christ in ourselves, the more we are apt to see him in others and the more we are able to see the subtle dangers (sin)
blocking the Spirit.

Self-awareness is also a prelude and companion to Christian power. This power is both based on love and steeped in
the spiritual renewal that comes from a continual self-examination:

To them I have revealed your name, and I will continue
to reveal it so that your love for me may live in them, and
I may live in them (John 17:26).

This spiritual revelation involves a balance between
thought and action. To think and not act leads to obsessive
rumination. To act without thinking results in blind impul-
siveness. Self-awareness helps develop balance; it is a difficult
activity designed to aid us on our journey home to find Christ
in ourselves and, in turn, in our community.

The place to which we go is not new, only our fresh perception of the warmth now available from the hearth in us.
T.S. Eliot aptly notes:

We shall not cease from exploration
And the end of all our exploring
Will be to arrive where we started
And know the place for the first time.

The "place" in ourselves that we seek to see anew is, of
course, the beauty and strength of Christ. We seek this not to
weep the tears of false consolation that flow when a poignant
movie ends happily; we seek this, instead, to be more in touch
with the hopeful faith that is needed to face the chilling challenges inherent in the mystery of our moving position in life.

The search, then, is for God's word within us, not so that
we might have power, but rather to enable ourselves to attest
to God's power over the world—including that special personal world, the one we call "the self."

Living a life of massive denial of the (sometimes ugly) real-
ities around us only postpones the anxiety of facing the truth
about ourselves and the world. At the end of life, having successfully avoided the Truth, we end up with an empty epitaph
and a history noteworthy only in the great amount of time
spent running away from the necessary pain and growth of life.

On the other hand, living an aware life means that we must face directly the crisis of reality. This stark event sometimes brings us to the brink of despair. It is the time that our hope is like a clenched fist holding on tightly to our faith, not daring to open our hand even for a second for fear of losing what little belief we think we have left . . . or, worse yet, frozen with the fear that we might look into our faith and find nothing left.

John Le Carré touches upon this theme dramatically when he speaks of crisis and courage in his novel *The Little Drummer Girl*:

> *There is no fear like it.* . . . Your courage will be like money. You will spend and spend, and one night you will look in your pockets and you will be bankrupt and that is when the real courage begins.[3]

Viewing self-awareness as an integral part of courageous faith development, we don't see it as a nicety brought about by a sensitivity training group. Nor do we see it as a way to become more successful, more wealthy, or better able to get what we feel we deserve out of life. Rather, it is, quite simply, a requirement for *survival*. By avoiding self-awareness we risk more than the failure to discern some possibly helpful knowledge . . . we risk losing everything!

With self-awareness and faith in Christ we can look out at the world with a sense of anticipation and vision. Concomitantly, our talents for more accurately perceiving who we are now will increase. In searching for clarity, we will begin to appreciate: the value of discipline, the rewards of uncovering inconsistencies or incongruent feelings or thoughts, and the special need for focus when trying to be introspective.

Discipline

Discipline is essential, because without a rhythm to self-reflection, the stamina needed to discern the progression of our personality pattern in light of the Gospel call is almost impossible. There is an often heard statement about prayer to the effect that "If you are too busy to pray, you are too busy." A similar sentiment can be expressed about Christian self-awareness. Failure to have our mental fingers continually on the pulse of where we are psychologically and spiritually is to deprive the center of our life's activity (prayer) from receiving essential, accurate nourishment to prepare it for relationship with God.

When we ask ourselves each day—for ten or fifteen minutes—what we feel affectively (sadness, happiness, depression?) and where we are cognitively (what are we thinking, perceiving, and understanding in response to today's experiences?), we bring self-awareness to life with Grace-full assertiveness. Similarly, when we are regularly attentive to the ebb and flow of our reactions, we are in an ideal position to gather the subtle inconsistencies which can provide us with a link to our preconscious. We will be able to discern clues to where we are now by picking up glints of mental material which might normally be just beyond our level of awareness.

Inconsistencies and a "Creative Synthesis"

Psychoanalytic and religious thinkers alike have long advised us to be alert to feelings and thoughts which seem to be incongruent. By reaching for them, we may be able to put needed new life into our possibly static pictures of ourselves. I find it easy to agree with such a sound point of view:

> Thinking or doing things that are generally out of character for us, or are not in line with our basic style of dealing with the world, should not be dismissed as irrelevant exceptions brought on by unusual circumstances. Instead they are hints of hidden elements. With them we need to seek a *creative synthesis* in understanding ourselves or we will be dismissing buried treasure which is of great potential psychoreligious value.[4]

In seeking a "creative synthesis" we are trying to be like the Good Shepherd. We are leaving the "ninety nine" (those consciously acceptable parts of our personality) to find and reconcile those seemingly alien parts of ourselves with the rest of our personality. In this light, knowing is not distressing, but the "entre" to being made more whole, more holy. Just as we seek solidarity in the global village with faces and customs strange to us, we also need to strive to bring peace and growth to the community within us. The movement to leave the narrow corner of our anxious inner world is clearly worth the effort.

Avoiding Vagueness

This searching out the dark, possibly creative, parts of ourselves is made more possible when time is taken out to focus on the specifics of our reactions. Focus helps us to undo "repression" and "suppression" (unconscious and conscious forgetting). By avoiding vagueness, which is brought about by efforts to remove seemingly unacceptable thoughts and impulses from consciousness, we can more easily involve ourselves with the material that lies just below the surface of our awareness.

By dealing directly, and as assertively as possible, with a specific issue or theme unearthed as a result of our day's interpersonal travels, the door is opened to greater awareness of where the Spirit is leading us and where our defenses are trying to divert us. So, by understanding a single area of focus (e.g., a seemingly incongruent reaction, thought, or impulse), we can set the stage to broaden rather than narrow our horizon.

Theologians tell us of the themes of different spiritual writers (e.g., Ignatius—obedience; Benedict—humility; Francis—poverty; Nouwen—peace), but are quick to add that by delving deeply enough into one school of spirituality, we are put into contact with the others. This is also what occurs when, in self-awareness, we attempt to discover what is at the basis of one daily encounter or reaction; in pursuing one lead, we begin to uncover an entire thematic style of living and responding (or avoiding) the Spirit. With such a vigorous hopeful search, balance and clarity in our lives then become more of a reality. And in searching for our own true identity (Christ in us) we find not only a narrowly-defined version of our own *ego;* we find the *Truth.*

† † †

1 Corinthians 2:10–16

God has revealed this wisdom to us through the Spirit. The Spirit scrutinizes all matters, even the deep things of God. Who, for example, knows a man's innermost self but the man's own spirit within him? Similarly, no one knows what lies at the depths of God but the Spirit of God. The Spirit we have received is not the world's spirit but God's Spirit, helping us to recognize the gifts he has given us. We speak of these, not in words of human wisdom but in words taught by the Spirit, thus interpreting spiritual things in spiritual terms. The natural man does not accept what is taught by the Spirit of God. For him, that is absurdity. He cannot come to know such teaching because it must be appraised in a spiritual way. The spiritual man, on the other hand, can appraise everything, though he himself can be appraised by no one. For, "Who has known the mind of the Lord so as to instruct him?" But we have the mind of Christ.

4

Clarity

As Jesus did in his ministry before he finally offered himself as the perfect sacrifice, the true Christian leader must travel a narrow winding and treacherous road between banality and crucifixion.

—M. Scott Peck[1]

Clarity helps us to face almost any issue or person and feel the force of the biblical injunction, "Be not afraid." It is at the source of a healthy attitude toward life. With clarity, our actions become psychologically sound and spiritually responsive. Yet most of us consciously and unconsciously avoid seeing the Light. This may sound ridiculous, since being clear is so akin to being fully aware, fully *alive*. However, the process involved in seeing life clearly requires a good deal of focused energy and often forces us to give up many of our nostalgic illusions.

Clarity is not something that can be limited. The same perceptive light that pierces the shroud that is preventing better understanding of others and God simultaneously shines through the darkness of the denials we make about our own nature, our own style of living. In seeing everything clearly then, we must, by definition of this encompassing process, see our own games as well. This is not something we are used to doing. We often hide things from ourselves, and unconsciously we certainly often try to deceive others. Father John Eudes alludes to this issue in two of the comments he makes to Henri Nouwen as recorded by Father Nouwen in his *The Genesee Diary*. The first of these reads:

This morning Father John explained to me that the killdeer is a bird that fools you by simulating injury to pull your attention away from her eggs which she lays openly on a sandy place. Beautiful! Neurosis as weapon! How often I have asked pity for a very unreal problem in order to pull people's attention away from what I didn't want them to see. [2]

Secondly, he says:

John Eudes made me see that the problem of obedience is a problem of intimacy. "Obedience becomes hard when you have to be vulnerable to the other who has authority. You can play the obedience game in such a way you never disobey any rule while keeping from your guide and director, your abbot or superior those things about which you do not want to hear a "no." You need a lot of trust to give yourself fully to someone else, certainly to someone to Whom you owe obedience. Many people adapt very quickly but are not really obedient. They simply don't want to make waves and instead go along with the trend. That is not obedience. That is just adaptation. [3]

Still, the effort to honestly face ourselves is essential. If we don't avoid or give up, if we don't panic when faced with the reality of our personal games, much personal restoration and power are possible. The point is that once we understand, we can accept; once we can accept, we can be open to being healed and open to the role we all have in healing others. What more can we ask of a process if it can produce such results? What better journey can we take if this be the ongoing reward of such a *quest*?

Being clear, then, is the act of gaining a Christian perspective on our life. This is a life in relationship: relationship with self, others, and God. Such a perspective will cause both tension and peace; such a perspective is also contextual—it is very much cradled in the past, present, and our view of the future. Finally, it requires the stamina, discipline, patience, humility, and courage to be a critical thinker in light of the Gospel and the exemplary ministry of Christ.

Obviously all of this is not easy. However, what choice is left? If we are to be available to others and God, we must be available to the Christ within us. And to accomplish this, we must try—at all cost—to be clear.

To be clear is to be close, very close to God. Just as we experience the Eucharist as Christ's physical presence, with this clarity we can almost touch Jesus when through Love he appears in ourselves and others. At such times we realize the promise of Jesus not to leave us orphaned (John 14:18), for we see his Spirit around us and within us.

From this clarity we can then be open to the gift of grace and the experience of "consolation" that Ignatius of Loyola speaks about with respect to our relationship with God. This is the promise of God; this is the result of clarity.

Seeking to be clear then is the only real journey. Other forays into life are really trips into fantasy, a luring fantasy but a fantasy nonetheless. This we shall see by looking at some of the elements surrounding the issue of clarity and its implications for the way we live each day.

The Context of Clarity

Clarity does not occur in a vacuum. It is inextricably bound to both personal *mission* and *vision*. Mission provides the basis and driving force for clarity, whereas vision provides the horizon which guides us, which leads us on each day . . . each year.

The incredible power of mission—especially when it is clear—is breathtaking. Charles Kingsley aptly notes:

We act as though
comfort and luxury
were the chief requirements
of life,
when all we need
to make us really happy
is something
to be enthusiastic about.

For the Christian, mission both precedes and is a product of clarity. To see reality for what it is, even when that reality includes our own lives, we have to own a mission which doesn't delude us from the beginning. For instance, if we see our reason for being as personal power or success, we can never have "Christian clarity" no matter how hard we try. Moving as fast as we can may temporarily allay our anxiety and convince us that we are "running the good race." Obviously if we are going in the wrong direction, the truth of the situation is that we are not progressing at all; we are just wasting time.

On the other hand, if our mission starts on a good footing by being tied to the call to be like Christ, mission then becomes a product of clarity. That is to say, in trying to be open to the Spirit, we are actually seeking on a daily basis to become more aware of what a Christian mission implies for us *now*.

Clarity then is actually another way of viewing *metanoia* (conversion). Initially conversion must come as a commitment to being Christlike, and, in this light, to be as fully ourselves as possible. Following this, conversion takes the form of a *continual* call to discern which is the false self, the false life, and which is the true self, the Way.

Vision adds to this by providing a worthy goal. It is a distant line that marks the meeting of the heavens (the transcendent God) and the earth (the Incarnate Word, Jesus); it is the future commingling of the unfulfilled hope and the possible presence of Christ in us in a more complete way. In this light, vision represents the future, not so much with respect to what I will own or what I will be doing, but instead it refers to who I will *be* . . . in Christ.

Goals of Clarity

Christian clarity has numerous specific goals. However, for our purposes the emphasis is on achieving perspective, being more aware of all of our agendas, appreciating what the serious risks of life are, and knowing the importance of critical thinking.

Perspective is a gifted outcome of clarity. Yet, achieving a sufficiently accurate perception of reality is obviously not easy. Perspective can be achieved in either a dramatic or a slow manner; the triggering factor in both cases, though, must be a commitment to embracing the world in an open gracious way. Otherwise, no amount of information—no matter how startling or obvious to most eyes—will break through our hard shells of resentment, preconceived notions, and self-determined expectations.

There is a famous Spanish proverb which says, "I complained because I had no shoes until I met a man who had no feet." Unfortunately, this proverb doesn't hold true for most of us. Blocking ourselves from seeing our good fortune is incredibly easy. Being grateful for life is something which requires conscious daily effort.

Several years ago, my daughter was hospitalized for severe scoliosis. She needed to have thirteen levels of her spine fused and a metal rod inserted for support. At twelve years of age, this was quite an ordeal for her (and her anxious parents). An unexpected positive result of this occurrence was the opportunity it provided for both my wife and me to gain perspective.

I still remember the initial impact of hearing that she had this problem. I had always been someone who was busy worrying about nonsense in the past and future while ignoring the essentials of the present. The following words by Henri Nouwen had taken root at some level but needed an emotional push to really become a force in my life. He said, "More enslaving than our occupation . . . are our preoccupations. To be preoccupied means to fill our time and place long before we are there. . . . It is a mind filled with 'ifs'."[4] If anything, my daughter's ordeal helped me grow toward recognizing not only that I was preoccupied with many things and not appreciating the joy of the present (my daughter's laugh, comments, interruptions) but also that many of the things I was preoccupied with were either trivial and/or beyond my control.

My wife, who also gained perspective from the event, described a specific incident which particularly opened her eyes. During the period immediately following surgery when we were both still rather anxious about our daughter's recovery, Michaele spent most of the day at the hospital. On one such day a young patient called to her from across the hall. When she looked to see who had called, she was greeted by the smiling face of a young woman in her late teens. This patient was in a cast extending from her collarbone to her ankles and lying flat on her stomach in a specially designed auto-controlled wheelchair.

When my wife walked across the hall the young woman asked her why she spent so much time at the hospital. Michaele explained that she was there to visit our daughter who had recently undergone spinal surgery. The young patient thought for a moment and then said, "Well, don't look so worried; I'm sure things will work out as best as they can." At first my wife felt a bit embarrassed, given the fact that this young woman, who was experiencing such an ordeal herself was the one reaching out to her with words of cheer. But then she recognized what a blessing those words were. The blessing? The unconditional appreciation of life as gift.

As my wife and I exchanged thoughts on how this difficult situation gave us a new perspective and brought us blessings we hadn't expected, we awaited a visit to our daughter by a friend of ours. This single attractive man has a good job, is bright and lives in a warmly furnished apartment in a nice suburb. Yet he feels dejected and most of the time he is a quite depressed character. As a matter of fact, when anyone tries to help him gain perspective, he indicates in some fashion that they "just don't understand." When something good happens to him, he thinks, "Too bad this has to pass so quickly."

As I looked around at the milieu I was in, namely a wonderful hospital where the staff is professional and caring, and the patients (all children) are so full of joy and acceptance of life—their lives, "handicaps" and all—my thought was, "I wonder how he will react when he comes in to visit." Well, he entered and I thought, "Surely, he will notice the love, the joy, the acceptance, and feel better about his own life." Instead, he said, "Doesn't all of this bother you? I know I can't stand looking at so many problems." He missed the accepting hearts of the children, was oblivious to the caring eyes of the nurses and therapists.

Perspective is something we must be open to, actively seek, and want to appreciate. It is a goal of clarity that we must constantly put before ourselves. It is a special blessing to be received over and over again if we are willing to embrace it. But more than that, it is intimately connected with *prayerfulness*. If we are grateful for the gift of each new day and have a conviction that each fresh day is the opportunity for a new encounter with God, perspective will come—even amidst pain. Archbishop Bloom puts this better than I can in his classic book, *Beginning To Pray:*

Awake in the morning and the first thing you do, thank God for it, even if you don't feel particularly happy about the day which is to come. . . . Once you have done this, give yourself time to realize the truth of what you are saying and really mean it—perhaps on the level of deep conviction and not of what one might call exhilaration. And then get up, wash, clean, do whatever else you have got to do and then come to God again. Come to God again with two convictions. The one is that you are God's own and the other is that this day is also God's own, it is absolutely new, absolutely fresh. It has never existed before. To speak in Russian terms, it is like a vast expanse of unspoiled snow. No one has trodden on it yet. It is all virgin and pure in front of you.[5]

Too often we miss clarity and we keep ourselves from gaining perspective because we prejudge the world. We decide what to be thankful for; we conclude what kinds of things in life can satisfy *our* sense of hope. Instead, what we really need to do is open our eyes to the full possibility of the total range of gifts that life has to offer us as God's own. In Brother David Steindl-Rast's words "The eyes of hope are grateful eyes. Before our eyes learned to look gratefully at the world, we expected to find beauty in good-looking things. But grateful eyes expect the surprise of finding beauty in *all* things."[6]

In working with persons studying to be pastoral counselors, I ask them to ask the ultimate question when they deal with people. They shouldn't just seek answers to the questions, "What is wrong with this client? What can I do to help this person?" They must also ask—it is really their primary question as *pastoral* counselors—"What is Jesus saying to me in this suffering person?" Only then will they be able to see the beauty amidst the pain. Only then will they be able to share perspective and clarity. For if we are not fully open to the mystery of life ourselves, how can we expect to help others with their lives? How can we expect to be open, to be available, to God?

Being aware of all of our agendas is also a function of the quest for Christian clarity. Too often there is a fear of looking at the many reasons we do things or a simplistic retreat into naively believing we do things for only one reason. In most cases there is a continuum of reasons. Some of them are conscious, others are dimly known or beyond our awareness. Some reasons for our actions are mature, others aren't. To understand our behavior and achieve clarity we have to attempt to be as aware of as many of our agendas as we can.

With effort it is possible to pick up many of the agendas that are dimly known or just beyond our level of awareness (preconscious). By reflecting on why we want to do something, have said something, or behaved in a particular way, we can both understand ourselves better and appreciate why people react to us the way they do.

The main block to examining our agendas is personal defensiveness. When people are taught to examine and explain their behavior to themselves and others, there is an implicit pressure to show that one acted in good faith, one acted altruistically, one was mature, one was "in the right." However, to gain clarity these rules must be suspended. There must be a realization that in all major and most minor decisions, actions and behaviors, there are usually a myriad of reasons—some of them quite immature—behind why we think, feel, or do something.

The problem doesn't arise when we have immature reasons; the problem comes to the fore when we avoid, deny and try to disguise them. The way progress is made is by uncovering immature agendas, for in doing so we allow room for our mature ones to grow.

For instance, with respect to people entering religious life or wanting to become a psychologist or psychiatrist, the initial (possibly unstated) reasons they do it may be status, power, voyeurism, security, or an effort to meet the expectations of others (e.g., parents). Personally, I believe this is the case to some degree in all people making a choice to enter these service professions. However, that is not the important issue. When people are screened to enter religious life or mental health work, immature reasons and goals are expected. The important differentiating factor is not whether or not they have only mature reasons; the distinguishing issue is whether or not they are healthy enough to grow out of the immature ones, and be able to nurture the mature ones.

In psychology, those who can't step beyond immaturity and still enter the field eventually become therapists who are either self-absorbed, narcissistic, and unable to develop as a helper (thus they merely continue to practice their mistakes rather than grow), or they become so disillusioned by the actual work involved in helping others face their emotional problems that they must leave the field—or, worse, become so disillusioned that they commit suicide.

In religious life, once the status wears off and there is a recognition that ministry is not a place to hide from the world but a place to confront it radically in line with the Gospel, the same kind of disillusionment or extreme behavior may also occur. However, for those mature and open enough to work through their difficulties and dashed unrealistic expectations (possibly with the help of colleagues, a counselor and/or spiritual guide), there is an opportunity for a naive and possibly faltering vocation to bloom into a wise, humble, and strong one.

The same can be said about the decision and actions taken by all of us on a daily basis. The more effort taken to understand our motivations and goals, the more we can learn about ourselves, our anxieties, and our needs. Questioning ourselves helps. Do we tread softly with someone because such a form of charity is needed at this point, or do we do it because we have a desperate need to be liked? Are we pushing this project because it would be good for the school, parish, institution, or company for whom we work, or is it because it will help us gain more power, be more famous?

Now in most cases, we generally do things for a number of reasons. Some of these reasons may be good ones while others may be tied directly to our own needs, anxieties, and so forth. In trying to achieve clarity we need to assertively look at all reasons—*not* merely as a means of purging ourselves of our less than pure reasons, but more as a means of understanding why we do things so that we can grow.

If we look at our behavior in an effort to purge our sinfulness, the process will be ill-fated from the start. We will be a vengeful god to ourselves and do nothing but depress and upset ourselves to the point that we may give up such an effort altogether or lose sight of our gifts and God's all encompassing love and forgiveness.

What we need to do is to clearly look at the mature reason and then try to figure out what other reasons we might have had. Then when we pick up the other reasons ("I was nice because I fear any form of disagreement"), we can ask ourselves why we are so concerned, afraid, etc., over this. We can also ask ourselves, "What is the worst thing that could happen if we did or said something different or we didn't get our way?" For example, if it is our desire to always do the right thing, what is the worst thing that would happen if someone misunderstood our behavior or approach? Suppose that someone did think ill of us or thought we weren't the best psychologist, the holiest minister, the most dedicated teacher. What of it?

Aren't there times when someone else is right? So what? The answer to this question may be that we are depending more on the views others have of us than the acceptance we count on from God. We are acting in spite of Jesus' crucifixion and trying to capture heaven on our own. Instead of trying to be virtuous because we want to position ourselves to receive the free gift of grace and instead of having a self-esteem that comes from knowing that God loves us and our own love of (Christ in) ourselves, we are trying in the instance cited above to get our successful identity from outside. This is the kind of information that comes from trying to be clear in identifying our agendas.

The goal is certainly worth it because not only does it help us perceive reality (including our attitudes and motivations) more clearly, but it frees us from the bonds of our own unnecessary anxieties and helps us face life directly and unafraid. But this takes effort; it takes a strong desire to break through our resistances to critical thinking.

Critical thinking requires stamina, discipline, patience, humility, openness, and *faith*. By faith I am not referring to a list of beliefs, but to a strong trust in the Lord. In the words once again of Steindl-Rast, "Faith was courageous trust in Jesus and in the good news which he lived and preached. Eventually this trust would crystallize into explicit beliefs, it is true. But the starting point is trusting courage, not beliefs. And in our life of faith—just as in lighting a fuse—it makes a vital difference at which end we start."[7]

With this courageous trust we try to emulate critical thinkers by seeking to ask ourselves the following types of questions:

1. Am I seeking to see things in black and white or am I willing to appreciate the ambiguity—the "grays"—of things?
2. Do I just seek answers, even in those areas where there are none to be had?
3. Do I try to see how my views of self, others, and God correspond to the reality of others? In other words, do I cri-

tique my attitudes and beliefs so that I don't slip into secure delusions?

4. Am I slow to believe and not subject merely to rhetoric or convenient conclusions? Am I able to hold onto the possible as well as the probable without pain?

5. Am I able to enter into the mystery of the unfolding of Jesus being revealed to me or am I looking for cookbook approaches to life?

6. Do I gravitate toward the quick solution or one side of an issue because I lack the intellectual stamina and solid theology of hope that encourages an open mind and an open heart?

7. Am I so afraid of failure and rejection by others that I go along with what opinion I perceive as current rather than the one I perceive as more in line with the Gospel? (Martin Luther King, Jr. said, "The ultimate measure of a man is not where he stands in moments of comfort and convenience, but where he stands at times of challenge and controversy. The true neighbor will risk his position, his prestige, and even his life for the welfare of others.")

8. Do I say I belong to the pilgrim Church but find dogma and doctrines my permanent oasis in a desert that I know Jesus wants me to venture out into as one of his followers?

9. Do I see my learning and theological education to be the responsibility of my leaders and guides, and not a matter of personal quest and conscience?

10. Am I truly open to a *repeated* conversion of my beliefs, my attitudes—my heart—or do I resist the disturbing chill of the fresh air that must come in when I open my heart and mind's door to the Spirit? More specifically, am I willing to examine unpleasant personal thoughts, impulses, and feelings so that I can find out more about myself and the direction I am moving in life? Once again, a few lines from

Henri Nouwen in *The Genesee Diary* might clarify this essential point:

> The most persistent advice of John Eudes in his spiritual direction is to explore the wounds, to pay attention to the feelings, which are often embarrassing and shameful, and follow them to their roots. He keeps telling me not to push away disturbing daydreams or hostile meanderings of the mind but to allow them to exist and explore them with care. Do not panic, do not start running, but take a careful look.[8]

This "careful look" is something that we are tempted to resist at all cost. Most of us feel secure amidst our denials, avoidances, suppressions, repressions, rationalizations, projections, and other defenses. We like to keep the anxiety that comes with facing ourselves and the fact we are going to die under check. We don't want to hear that we don't have control over our own destiny.

There is a great price to pay for this illusion, though. As long as we refuse to face ourselves as we are, we will not be able to "rest in the Lord." Though we may delude ourselves into moments of calm distraction, each day the reality of our false journey and denials will seep through because we know who we are. In the words of James Finley,

> Promethean man is man aware of the mystery of his solitude. An owl sitting alone in the forest at night is not lonely. The owl is the forest. The blackness of the night is his mother. He preens his feathers, needing no one to observe or comment upon his solitary beauty. But a man alone in the forest at night is lonely indeed. The blackness of the night is not his mother but a mirror of his own solitude—a vast unknown expanse of nothingness which he

both carries about within him and stands before like a stranger.[9]

The choice is simple—but admittedly hard. We can move through life as if nothing but "getting ahead" and some religious awareness or practices are sufficient. The advantage: we don't have to take the time to look at ourselves honestly and openly; we don't have to disturb anything. The disadvantage: we will always be aware we are missing something—more than something, the element that can make us feel complete. Thus, we will always be anxious and prey to what people think, what we own, what we have accomplished in our eyes and the eyes of others.

The other choice: we can look at ourselves, *not* in front of an angry God, but in front of a loving God in whose presence we stand always, whether we admit it or not. The advantage: we will be open to a life of true gratitude, a life with meaning and purpose. The disadvantage: we will have, in Rahner's words, to leave the temporary security fed by our own denials and that of others avoiding reality and move out of "our little huts into (God's) night."[10]

This choice is up to us. We don't make it once, although we can probably recognize one or several dramatic moments when it was or was not made. We make it every day. And when it is made in favor of clarity, true clarity, then we are open to God and in a position to be in real solidarity with others. Availability to ourselves increases along with availability to God and others because there is a unity in being true to oneself, others and God. It is commonly referred to as "The Truth and The Way."

† † †

Luke 6:39–42

Jesus used images in speaking to them: "Can a blind man act as a guide to a blind man? Will they not both fall into a ditch? A student is not above his teacher; but every student when he has finished his studies will be on a par with his teacher.

"Why look at the speck in your brother's eye when you miss the plank in your own? How can you say to your brother, 'Brother, let me remove the speck from your eye,' yet fail yourself to see the plank lodged in your own? Hypocrite, remove the plank from your own eye first; then you will see clearly enough to remove the speck from your brother's eye."

II

Being Available to . . . Others

Introduction

The previous section pointed out that having a good relationship with ourselves becomes more and more possible when we are willing to embark on a serious journey. This journey is one in which we seek to cut away our "psychological brush," to see ourselves for who we really are, and for who we are truly meant to be. Such availability to the Christian self is naturally not easy. However, by appreciating our uniqueness, by embracing our failures in the midst of a certitude that we are forgiven, and by making a daily decision to seek self-awareness through a commitment to clarity, we can see that such availability to ourselves is still possible.

All of these efforts to find God within ourselves are actually ways in which we "knock on the door" of the kingdom. They are cries to Christ to grant us entry. Only he can be our door, and we use our efforts at the stewardship of ourselves as an acknowledgment of this reality. Stewardship of self is so inextricably bound up with stewardship of others, though, that being available to ourselves is never really possible if we are not also open and sensitive to other people. And so, with this in mind we now address the issue of availability to *others*.

Being with Christ means being with him in ourselves and others simultaneously. The Spirit in us dies if we cut ourselves off from others (the body of Christ); this part is obvious to most of us but there is actually more to it than this. The increase in our availability to ourselves *depends* on an increase in our availability to others. I am not speaking here about a narrowly compulsive, desperate, or duty-bound entry into others' lives. Instead, it is an actual search for Jesus amidst the turmoil and joy of other people that is needed.

Yet, given this, in a world of so many people and numerous demands, the following questions come to mind about our openness to others: Where do we start? How do we relate? What do we do with the rejection and pain we encounter? How does our availability to others increase our availability to ourselves? (The concept sounds paradoxical.)

The key to these questions is not found merely in the good communication skills of psychology or the tenets of current theology—although both of these are certainly helpful for community living. The key, quite simply, is *Jesus*. In both the upcoming chapter on "Relationships" and in the one entitled "Their Pain, Our Fears," the undercurrent is the constant search for the presence of the Lord. The most basic question is: How am I being Jesus to others *and* where is the Lord present in others? In this question the "and" should never become an "or." When unconsciously or consciously we focus solely on ourselves or others, we run the risk of losing our way. In such an instance we may become pedantic helpers or wind up being victimized ourselves to the point of a depletion of our resources.

Being available to others is not just giving time, money, and effort. It is also not endlessly worrying about others so that our personal tension rises to the point that we are overloaded and have no energy to care about anything or anyone anymore. After all, what would such imprudent masochism prove? Instead, being really available to others is being creatively alive for, and with, them. The true goal, which unfortunately often gets distorted or lost, is to share the Lord with others while in turn looking for and enjoying his sometimes almost-hidden presence as it is revealed in them.

After visiting drought-ridden Ethiopia, Senator Edward Kennedy said that when the half-starved children were brought into the rescue stations their eyes lacked the luster of a desire to live. However, after receiving some nourishment over a period of days, they would come to life again. Not only would their eyes brighten but the playfulness would return to their attitude; their bodies would smile again. The bread that had renewed their lives also had opened up the possibility for them to be interested in loving life once again.

This is the sense of aliveness we must seek for others; this is the sense of aliveness we must also seek for ourselves—not in saying a lot of words to people, not in completing a compulsive list of works, and not in trying to respond to everyone's expectations (including our own!), but in trying, with all of our being, to develop an attitude of openness and alertness in our interactions with others which is based on only one thing: the desire to look for and bring Christ *everywhere*.

5

Relationships

The language that God hears best is the silent language of love.

—*St. John of the Cross*

The potential psychological power and spiritual strength of a relationship is amazing. Like a bright fire it can help illumine the truth when we feel in the dark, instantly warm us when we feel alone, and blind and distort our vision when we get close enough to be burned or almost consumed by it. Deny it or not, involve ourselves in one or not, a relationship has inherent powers for both good and evil.

The importance of relationships has long been emphasized in psychology. The work on interpersonal sensitivity and group dynamics is now voluminous. From a theological perspective, deep concern with relationships has also been present; a relationship has always been a place where the Spirit of Jesus can and should be found and experienced. Although narrow forms of spiritualism (e.g., "quietism") have sometimes tried to distort the importance of seeking out God in relationships, serious theologians have been quick to call us back to the truth of the Gospels. They have pointed out time and again the clear basis for valuing our communal movement toward and with God. For instance, Karl Rahner noted that in recent years Catholics in particular have fallen into the mentality of so emphasizing the "single ultimacy of God that they neglect God's intrinsic community."[1] Quite simply, we can't approach salvation alone. The issue of God and the issue of community are inseparable.

45

Consequently, there is no doubt about the psychological and theological basis for interest and involvement in relationships. Denying that we are all part of the global village or drawing back into our insularity is obviously an absurd style of living to seek or defend. However, knowing that we should open ourselves up to meet God in our relationships is one thing. Facing the reality of the problems that arise from personal interactions and efforts at intimacy is quite another!

So distressful can interpersonal relations be that some people almost completely withdraw from the world as a way of self-preservation. For others, the road taken is completely the opposite. In cases like these, clinging, choking neediness or aggression occurs until the relationship is embattled, embittered, or gone.

For most of us though, there is a desire to somehow take a less dramatic path. Somehow we plod through in our efforts to relate to others the best way we can. Yet, despite the use of an approach that is usually successful, we too must somehow find solutions to the stress under which relationships put us. Unfortunately, when we try to do this, among the more common methods of handling the pains of growing interpersonally which we are tempted to use are the defenses which shift the focus of the sources of any difficulties we have in relating onto the other people involved.

The tendency in this instance is not to see ourselves as being a major part of the dynamics involved when strain arises in our relationships. W.H. Auden points out, "It is, for example, axiomatic that we should all think of ourselves as being more sensitive than other people because, when we are insensitive in our dealings with others, we cannot be aware of it at the time: conscious insensitivity is a self-contradiction."[2]

Probably the best tip-off to such projections of blame is the fact that we see things in black-and-white terms and we tend to deem ourselves the victim.

- "I've about had it! That's the last time I help them out or speak up." (We feel unappreciated.)
- "I'm always there for them but ask them for one favor and it's as though you're asking for the world." (We feel exploited.)
- "Every time the weekend comes everybody seems to have something to do but me. I'm a nice person. Why don't they like me?" (We feel left out.)

When we give the blame away we feel a sense of self-justification and relief that it's not our fault, and then we don't have to look at and own part of the cause for failure. However, the problem arising from this approach is that in giving away the blame we also give away the *power*. After all, if the people in our environment are the source of our interpersonal problem, then there is little we can do but move away from them and try to find new people with whom to interact. (And, unfortunately, in community living this sometimes really seems to be the only solution.) If it is something partially within our own attitude and behavior and is coming from something within our own relationship with ourself, then the interpersonal difficulty is at least within striking distance of improvement through our own self-understanding and subsequent actions.

Another problem with projection is that we may dismiss the information others give us that might be helpful if we took the time to really listen to it. Interpreting others' actions or comments too self-referentially without reviewing them critically enough can prevent us from understanding situations for what they are. For instance, when others seem angry with us and we say too quickly that it is totally *their* problem, we may miss some helpful information as to how we might be behaving defensively. Also, if we say that it is solely their problem we may subsequently shy away from them and miss a potentially good relationship or an opportunity to overcome the prejudices we are all taught early in life. Yet, if we fight this tendency to project, and also try to be impassioned and objective in the examination of our interactions, and trust that as persons we are all right (loved and love-able), we can look to see what is to be learned from our role in the interpersonal problems we are experiencing.

In doing this we may learn that the problem has practically nothing to do with us and be able to assess what the other person is doing and what, if anything, we can do. For example, if the person is actually trying to victimize us for some reason, we can ask why. Then without undue anger or fear on our part we can seek to clear up and/or extricate ourselves from the situation. Whatever outcome we choose, though, if the decision is to be a psychologically healthy and spiritually sound one, we must first attempt to remove our own anxieties and defensiveness so that we can be clear. Clarity about our relationships with others is dependent on the type of relationship we have with ourselves.

The victimization of ourselves by other people is not possible unless we victimize ourselves first by not relating to ourselves in a healthy fashion. When we neither trust ourselves nor love ourselves enough to believe that it is all right to make a mistake, be misunderstood, have people think ill of us, or have someone be angry at us (for a good reason or not), then we are asking for trouble with respect to how we perceive and interact with others. When we fail to move in the direction of good self-awareness out of a deep sense of trust that we are worthwhile, we can't examine our style of dealing with others (especially the mistakes we make), and our relationships will only become mere negotiations on our part to get what we believe we need out of life—even though we may clothe it in a pseudo-Christian guise of self-sacrifice or righteous indignation.

The choice is up to us: knowing ourselves and participating in open healthy and challenging relationships, or running away from a recognition of our destructive needs, anxieties, and insecurities and thus setting ourselves up to involve ourselves in "safe," overly dependent, or possibly "sick" relationships.

If we want to visit new lands we can't just sit in our living rooms and expect it to happen. Poring over even the best travel logs can't give us an experience anywhere near the ones we'd get while slowly walking along the Tiber on a sunny spring day, or rushing around London in the rain. Similarly, if we want to see God in ourselves and others we must be open. *We will only find the Spirit if we are open to the spiritual part of ourselves that lies hidden under our fears and are open to the special opportunity that lies beyond our presently safe relationships in those people we haven't met yet and in those existing friends who call us to be more than we are now.*

God's presence is being unfolded in the world today, but when we shy away from the challenges of an open relationship with ourselves and others, we are wasting time and behaving as those who stood around looking up at the sky for God while missing the Spirit who was filling the very space in which they stood (Acts 1:1). Who among us if given the opportunity to see God would say "no." Yet, isn't that what we are saying when we avoid the Truth as it is unfolded in the potential of our own growing self-awareness and our relationships with others?

The problem is, in the words of Israel Baal Shem: "The world is full of wonders and miracles but man takes his little hand and covers his eyes and sees nothing." The answer is that we need only believe, really believe, that God is here now and is continually being revealed in a new way in relationships. Based on this firm belief, then, we should take the time and pain to open our eyes and hearts to others.

Open to Self, Open to Others

Relationships are beneficial when they are open and free. The more conditioned they need to be, the less healthy and mature they are. The limits we place on others, and the ones we feel we must respond to from others, are often really unnecessary and destructive. There is a temptation to fool ourselves into believing that certain conditions are merely understandable expectations. Yet in our hearts we can recognize the fallacy of this by the negative feelings and tensions they engender. Any relationship that can't be trusted is not worth having.

Henri Nouwen during his Genesee experience came to this in his appreciation of how easy it is to limit and distort even the most beautiful interpersonal experience open to us, the one we call "love." He said, "It is important for me to realize how limited, imperfect, and weak my understanding of love has been. . . . My idea of love proves to be exclusive: 'You only love me truly if you love others less'; possessive: "If you really love me, I want you to pay special attention to me'; and manipulative: 'When you love me, you will do extra things for me.' Well, this idea of love easily leads to vanity: 'You must see something very special in me'; to jealousy: 'Why are you now suddenly so interested in someone else and not in me?' and to anger: 'I am going to let you know that you have let me down and rejected me.' "[3]

Opening up a place in our hearts for others so that we might be available to them, and in turn be gracious enough to appreciate the warmth of their gifts of self, is a difficult mystery of living. Because as people we tend to be so needy, there are so many nuances of openness that can be violated without our even knowing it. In the words of Thomas Hora, "To be interested is to love and revere; to be inquisitive, however, is to intrude, trespass, violate."[4] To have healthy relationships with others, we must be clear as to what is our relationship with ourself. The relationship with self determines how we deal with the world and how we view ourselves.

View of self and the world at large is unique to each person. No matter how much someone likes or hates us, knows or is unfamiliar with us, no one will ever view us or the world quite the same way we do. The reason for this is that we are unique. In psychological terms, we each have a singular feature called "the personality."

So, to understand our relationships with others there must first be an appreciation of how we relate to ourselves. If we are relaxed with ourselves, we will be at ease with others. If we feel insecure in terms of our own self-esteem, we will constantly be comparing ourselves to others. Relationship with self goes hand-in-hand with relationship with others. Pope John XXIII noted, "Whoever has a heart full of love always has something to give."

Our first relationships set the stage for the way we now feel about (or relate to) ourselves. Our parents and/or the significant people in our lives contribute to the way we feel about ourselves in two major ways. The first is obvious; namely, how they treated us. The messages they gave us in this respect had a major impact on the way we feel about ourselves today. Since nobody's parents are perfect, we all received messages at certain times which were more or less negative. They may not have been consciously malicious ones, but they served to make us doubt ourselves and look for affirmation in some way that we were "all right" as individuals. Some of us received these messages under the guise of being corrected, so now we may often be concerned whether we are doing the right thing or not. Some of us might have received the message that our style of dealing with the world was not in keeping with the norms of society as our family saw it. As a result, we may often be invested in trying to ensure we are saying and doing things in a way that won't draw attention or cause embarrassment.

The second element in our interactions with the significant figures in our early life that could have an adverse impact on us is not such an obvious one. It is the anxiety our parents or guardians had about themselves. Surprisingly, although these anxieties might have been communicated indirectly to us they can still be quite strong influences in our lives today. Therefore, as well as being taught insecurity through our lessons in growing up, we also learned them very subliminally in how we picked up the nuances from our own parents or guardians with respect to their own issues surrounding self-esteem.

These early influences are quite important, especially when we realize that these messages were given even preverbally—i.e., before we as very young children could understand and verbalize a spoken language. Also, since in most cases the messages were not given in a malicious conscious way, but inadvertently as a by-product of our parents' own humanness, they are hard to clearly see and address in ourselves now. It is almost as if we feel inadequate at times but don't see the cause for it.

The next major influence comes when we as children moved from the politics of the home to the politics of the world at large. At this time we began to test our styles of dealing with the world and also to see what people thought of us by how they treated and reacted to us. In doing this we not only got another chance—especially in the turbulent formative adolescent years—to examine and improve our self-image and self-esteem, but we began to recognize that some of our negative feelings didn't go away. Moreover, we saw that some of the people we dealt with seemed to reinforce our self-doubts by what they did or, more correctly, by what we perceived they did in response to our presence.

As adults now, we continue to do what we can to eliminate these self doubts. We may try to be very nice and win over the world. We may try to accomplish a great deal to impress the world. We may try to become witty in order to entertain and distract the world (including ourselves) from our possible insecurities. In other words, we build up a defensive style to prevent ourselves from being anxious that we aren't good enough and to convince others to help us believe that we are, at least in their eyes, all right.

For most of us, the style seems to work most of the time. As a matter of fact it becomes so successful as a personality style that we use it in most situations. However, we begin to recognize that our efforts at personality development in order to achieve others' affirmation cannot of themselves remove all of our personal doubts. In some cases, even when we do receive praise, the goal we seek is not completely achieved; we are not free. The reason is that, in looking to others to such an extent to make us feel sufficient as persons, we inadvertently simultaneously are setting ourselves up to become very dependent in the future on such positive feedback. The whole process becomes a vicious circle.

The self-esteem crisis, or opportunity, depending upon our point of view, comes when we decide that trying to work out the unfinished business of childhood through winning the approval of others just doesn't work. The recognition we finally get is that the flame of self-esteem must be fired from *within*. Interactions with others can fan the good things we feel about ourselves (e.g., through praise, positive feedback, acceptance). In these instances, however, we may be setting ourselves up to be addicted to the fanning of our ego by others to the point of exploitation of or extreme dependence on them.

At this point in our lives we have a choice: to continue to try to build up a resume of traits and accomplishments in the eyes of others with the false but occasionally reinforced belief that somehow we will feel good enough about ourselves some-day to feel absolutely secure, *or* to risk trusting that we are already worthwhile and are now really a special part of the unfolding of the universe.

If we aren't willing to let go of our games, we will have relationships built primarily on neediness, immaturity, and a pure desire to receive (albeit almost surreptitiously at times) rather than share—whereas, if we are willing to let go of this futile search to complete an impregnable edifice of self-esteem and if we are willing to deal with the occasional anxiety and panic that people won't like us if we don't play our pleasing or status-seeking games, we will be open to being "just ourselves," and freely bring Jesus to others while in turn be in a position to experience the Spirit in them.

Does this mean that in lowering our defenses we are being called to be another person and to throw away our personality style? Are we being asked to behave in a radically different way? No. The need is to change our attitude, our *motivations*. The goal is to stop running away from our false fears (anxieties) and to stop spending unnecessary energy running toward building up a false self designed to impress our real or imagined critics (including the ones we carry in our "heads" [e.g., our inner voices of self criticism] who represent our worst evaluators).

So, if we are now seen as nice people because we are easy to get along with, such a lovely style should certainly be kept. However, the motivation to be nice should not be based on an inappropriate fear of what people will think of us or how they will react. Such passivity will only cause anger and resentment in us and not be true to the image of the Lord within who deserves the respect that leads to questioning those who would treat us as "doormats." Rather, the gentle style should be used for a positive reason and a positive reason only—because we care.

Likewise, those of us who have tried to compete with the world, doing impressive things as a way of trying to overcome our feelings of inadequacy, should continue to try accomplishing things in the world. Yet, such accomplishments should not be exhibitionistic or competitive but should lie in the realm of enthusiasm. We should continue because burying our talents is foolish. At the same time, we are being alert not to involve ourselves in activities solely as a way of demonstrating that we are better at investing ourselves in the world than others. What errors lie in our personality style can be corrected when we have a good purpose underlying our behavior.

Whatever personality style we have, the goal is the same: *evolution*. We need to see what our personality style is, make it work, face those instances when it doesn't (e.g., look at those interpersonal situations when we become inordinately anxious and ask ourselves why we are making ourselves feel that way, instead of quickly blaming someone else), and take steps not to trip over our own personality by falling prey to believing we can raise our self-esteem through winning over the opinions of others. The belief must be that self-acceptance coming from embracing the fact that God created each one of us specifically in love is the only thing that can help us achieve feelings of self-worth. Others' love can aid in this process, but it cannot replace the necessity to continually nurture self-love and our recognition (through this) of God's love for us.

Coming out of this philosophy we can enter into relationships not with a sense of desperation and neediness but with a sense of hope and creativity. Our goal is changed from seeking what we can get, to seeking what further revelation of God we can uncover together with them.

With such a sense of availability to others as this, the way we view even our apparent interpersonal failures changes. With an attitude tied to a strong belief in God's love for us, the types of questions we ask move away from the realm of self-

blame or projection to self-understanding and a clear understanding of others; no longer do we fall as often into absolute
thinking ("Who's wrong here? Me or the other person?"). Instead we seek to figure out what is occurring, not as a means
to assign blame, but as a way to find God in the mystery of the
struggle.

Conflicts are natural. People disagree. We let people
down. They disappoint us. Jealousy occurs. Anger rises. And
depression coming from overgeneralizing negative events happens. These are all human problems. They are not going to
disappear in our lifetime. But we can begin to transform them.
They are mini-crises, and crises are, in part, an opportunity.
What we do with that opportunity is up to us.

Martin Buber said, "He who loves brings God and the
world together." What better place for this to happen than in
a relationship? What better way to give this a chance to happen
than to meet other people out of a strong belief that we are
loved, and a firm commitment to clearly examine those instances when we begin to become anxious and doubt it? The
door to relationships may seem locked by our anxious fear of
rejection, exploitation, ridicule, misunderstanding, and loss.
Still, with Love as the key and Christ as the door, certainly we
can begin to face others in a more healthy fashion—not with
interpersonal gimmicks that we always seem to forget and expectations that never seem to be met, but with an attitude of
hope that knows with strong faith that love is the surprise we
can always expect to somehow appear even in those gifts of relationship that seem impossible to open.

† † †

1 Corinthians 13:1–7, 13

Now I will show you the way which surpasses all the others.

If I speak with human tongues and angelic as well, but do not have love, I am a noisy gong, a clanging cymbal. If I have the gift of prophecy and, with full knowledge, comprehend all mysteries, if I have faith great enough to move mountains, but have not love, I am nothing. If I give everything to feed the poor and hand over my body to be burned, but have not love, I gain nothing.

Love is patient; love is kind. Love is not jealous, it does not put on airs, it is not snobbish. Love is never rude, it is not self-seeking, it is not prone to anger; neither does it brood over injuries. Love does not rejoice in what is wrong but rejoices with the truth. There is no limit to love's forbearance, to its trust, its hope, its power to endure. . . .

There are in the end three things that last: faith, hope, and love, and the greatest of these is love.

6

Their Pain, Our Fears

[In walking the streets of Calcutta] the poverty so en-
raged me that I wanted to scream at God. Then I came
to a painful realization. In the suffering of the poor,
God was screaming at me.

—*Jack Nelson*[1]

I don't know what your destiny will be,
but one thing I know,
the only ones among you who will be really happy
are those who have sought and found how to serve.

—*Albert Schweitzer*[2]

The literature of the early 1980's clearly reflected the dif-
ferences between ordinary concern and Christian compassion.
Secular psychology and psychiatry journals and books spoke
pointedly about the phenomenon of "burnout." The term became so overused that even those feeling mentally fatigued
from reaching out to others were sick of hearing the word.

"Burnout" literature stressed how helpers were prone to
personal depletion of enthusiasm and gave ways to avoid advanced stages of stress and depression which might be a partial
result of intense involvement in helping activities. As men-
tioned in the chapter on "Failure and Forgiveness" this information was quite helpful but it didn't go far enough. It lacked
an appreciation of the importance of a sound theology of hope.
Such a theology is not merely an extra resource for those dedicated to reaching out to others in pain, it is essential for our
very survival!

When hope based on the resurrection of Christ is not present, discouragement and despair appear and inevitably fan our feelings of futility. In such instances, we can misunderstand those in need of our help and can fail to see accurately our role with those under various forms of stress and injustice. We not only run the risk of failing to see God's role in saving the world, but also risk not seeing our own solidarity with the poor, the distressed, and the troubled. Instead, we see ourselves as "saviors." Everything is on our shoulders. We are "successful missionaries" reaching *down* to the sea of the needy. Is it any wonder that many of us shy away from helping? If we see our own visible results and inner feelings of accomplishment with the "less fortunate" as the only yardstick for our commitment to Christian helping, our continual involvement in daily ministry is doomed from its inception.

Fortunately, in addition to the secular material on burnout which helps us learn how to avoid unnecessary martyrdom through employing some psychological common sense, books which rely on a theology of hope and failure are also available to help Christians gain a perspective of the helping process and the attitude which is at its heart. The following quote from *Compassion* is one clear example of this:

> Here we are touching the profound spiritual truth that service is an expression of the search for God and not just of the desire to bring about social change. This is open to all sorts of misunderstandings, but its truth is confirmed in the lives of those for whom service is a constant and uninterrupted concern. As long as the help we offer to others is motivated primarily by the changes we may accomplish, our service cannot last long. When results do not appear, when success is absent, when we are no longer liked or praised for what we do, we lose the strength and motivation to continue. When we see nothing but sad, poor, sick, or miserable people who, even after our many attempts

to offer help remain sad, poor, sick, and miserable, then the only reasonable response is to move away in order to prevent ourselves from becoming cynical or depressed. Radical servanthood challenges us, while attempting persistently to overcome poverty, hunger, illness, and any other form of human misery, to reveal the gentle presence of our compassionate God in the midst of our broken world.[3]

Preparing To Help: Nurturing an Attitude of Compassion

To be compassionate on a continual basis requires the embrace of an attitude of openness to the potential that is inherent in any situation in which we reach out to others. This "potential," when it is *not* keyed simply to the act of giving to others in expectation of receiving a reward in terms of gratitude or great results, becomes a mysterious gift to be unwrapped in the act of searching for God in situations involving others. To see this gift our attitude must be one of a person undertaking a fresh, serious search for something valuable, something special that we have not yet found in the previously familiar persons in our environment, or something unknown and hidden in and behind the unfamiliar people and cultures of our city and our world.

Our attitude must also be one of ruthless resolution based on a trusting faith. In calling upon Jesus we must move *with* him into situations of suffering and not lag behind because of trembling doubts or personal pain. Meeting Jesus in prayer can bring peace and strong joy, but this doesn't mean that all anxiety and difficulties cease. In the following words of Robert Faricy we see that this is far from the reality we should expect. He says: "They make fun of Jesus for his weakness in the very hour that the power of God in Jesus saves the world. The saving and healing power of God cannot be dissociated from the cross of Jesus."[4] In being compassionate we should expect no less to happen to us.

Too often we pray for the inner healing of our doubts, our "unfinished business" with people, our hurts, and the voracious, personally consuming needs we have convinced ourselves must be filled now if we are to be happy. We may feel we pray for this healing so we can be courageously compassionate. However, in looking at the expectations of these prayers, there is often a sense of anticipation that God will somehow heal us by moving ahead of us to take on all of the hurts while we trail behind protected and unaffected. The reality is that we do need to ask Jesus to join us, but this joining should take the form of his walking with us in faith; we act in his name and deal with the pain *together*. We move forward in unison with strength and expectation. The expectation is that in reaching out to others we will be able to achieve solidarity with them in our hearts, so that their pain will be our pain, and our fears will cease to separate us from them—and from the Christ that is in their midst.

Our attitude must be a prayerful one too. It must be one that meets the sounds of sickness with the strength derived from solitude with God. Reaching out and helping others without such a prayerful base is playing with fire. With a dependence on God our commitment to others can result in our fears being chastened by the burning sadness of poverty, anger, depression, and anxiety, whereas if we go it alone, we may be almost consumed by the near despair of the world to the point of personal apathy, cynicism, or callousness.

The temptation to avoid or curb our efforts with those in pain is a "natural" one. It is our nature to stay away from the unpleasant, or to retreat when we feel we are failing or not being appreciated. And, unfortunately, the illustrations of negative experiences are not hard to find in the lives of concerned dedicated people everywhere in the world:

- A pastoral counselor who has seen ten clients for counseling is tired at the end of the day. She notices that the hour is up for her last client. With this she moves slightly forward in her chair. To this, the client shouts, "I know you have to throw me out after the hour is up, but you don't have to be so abrupt about it!" and storms out of the room.

- A priest spends a good deal of time trying to get a job for an ex-addict. He brings him back to his room, sees that he gets fed and arranges temporary housing. After one of the ex-addict's visits to the priest's room, the priest finds that the ex-addict has carefully rifled his room and stolen what few valuables he had.

- A volunteer community services worker in a geriatric center/soup kitchen gets up early to prepare breakfast for the aged and the homeless before she goes to her salaried job. One day she is surprised when the normal delivery of breakfast food doesn't occur due to a delivery van being in an accident. As she explains to some of the arriving people, they become abusive and accuse her of lying or incompetence.

- A parochial school teacher tries to explain to a parent why her child should remain in the same grade because of his emotional immaturity. To this suggestion, the mother responds by bitterly accusing her of being a poor teacher.

As we all know, the list is endless. The pressures are great in daily ministry.

Admittedly, there is no question that true ministry calls us to action and commitment; indeed, we must be active to relieve others from their misery and prevent unnecessary suffering. And no one would disagree with the statement that we should be concerned about the specific sorrows of others.

However, the important point emphasized here is that without a prayerful attitude tying us to God's saving power, and tethering us as well to other Christians, we as actively committed persons will find it hard to last under the pressures inherent in helping others. Therefore, prayer is not a nicety but actually is an essential for the survival of anyone committed to Christian ministry. To forget this is to open oneself to the serious dangers of inner fragmentation and a depletion of personal enthusiam.

Caring Presence

To help others see God in our actions we must also nurture our caring presence so that people can actually feel Jesus' warmth. After all, who makes us feel better—the person anxious to do all kinds of things for us, or the person who quiets our fearful pain with a smile, gives us a few moments of his or her time, and cheerfully offers us some reassuring actions of assistance? I wonder if that is not one of the little messages hidden in the New Testament story of Martha and Mary? Caring is clearly felt when the smile of love is not lost in the frenzy of so-called "efficient accomplishments."

The Ibo of Nigeria have a proverb that says, "It is the heart that gives; the fingers just let go."[5] Certainly, actions speak louder than words, but if actions don't flow out of an attitude fashioned by a trust in God and reflect Jesus' warmth, the source of the movements we make will soon lose heart and stop or become mechanistic. Look at the faces of people in nursing homes when someone stops, sits down, and speaks with them for a few minutes. They light up. What greater proof do we need of what kind of reaching out to others is really beneficial? The calm, attentive hand always heals more deeply than the quick touch of the busy "do-gooder."

To be really available to others is to open our hearts to them while looking for the Lord in their midst. To do this we don't bring ourselves and our busyness; we bring the awareness of God that we can only receive in prayer; it is in the forefront of our commitment. Yet, to do this requires alertness—fed by being attuned to questions such as the following:

- Am I willing to risk being compassionate? Am I willing to bear with those suffering their pain even though I may feel helpless, unappreciated, or anxious?

- Am I willing to bring the interior peace of my prayer life and share it with others, not necessarily in words, but by focusing on their needs and temporarily forgetting my own?

- Am I willing to be humble enough to see Jesus in the poor, the lowly, the sick, the depressed, and the anxious? Am I willing to let them finish their comments or statements to me even when I feel they are wrong or I think they do not know what they are talking about? In essence, am I willing to learn from them, not just about them?

- Am I willing to be patient—patient even when those I am ministering to don't seem to understand or like me? Can I be patient when the emotional bridge I build to others falls down each time I leave them and has to be rebuilt each time I return?

- Am I willing to be accepting of myself when I fail, or when I realize I am inadvertently trying to manipulate others, or when I get angry, want to retreat, or get depressed?

- Am I willing to try to open myself to the world of others by listening attentively to their words, their questions, their feelings, their needs? To do this, am I willing to withhold judgement and listen even if the manner of presenting their comments is negative, frightening, boring, puzzling, or seemingly too challenging for me?

• Am I willing to try to discern the expectations God has of me? Can I risk not meeting my own expectations or the ones others have of me? Am I willing to have the courage to risk being misunderstood?

• Am I willing to risk believing that my presence itself can be healing and not submit to the interior or exterior pressures to try to rush in with a quick "solution," or efficient action? Am I willing to help in the name of Christ and not worry that I am not the savior myself?

Careless Christianity

Questions such as the ones above can move us toward being "one with the Lord," toward being compassionate people. When this occurs we move more in the direction of responsiveness to the Spirit and less in the misdirection of becoming over-responsible. The goal is to avoid being so busy carrying inappropriate burdens that we don't have a free hand to carry the burdens that are meant for us. Thus, in being compassionate we are asked to be good stewards of our daily schedule. James Whitehead in an article on "An Asceticism of Time" notes, "Christian time management, as an asceticism, will always be understood as a response to grace, to the invitation to become less scattered and more aware of the Present already there. . . . Distress often arises not from doing bad, nor failing to act, but, intriguingly, from doing too much good."[6]

In his paper he goes on to point out that the need for us to shape our time is based on an appreciation of a Christian tradition which doesn't measure self-worth in terms of a compulsive listing of how busy we are, but instead calls us to discern what is and isn't essential so that we can be available to others when really needed.

The basic maxim is: When we respond to God we are free to suffer when it is necessary; when we respond to ourselves or are enslaved by a fear of not meeting the expectations of others, we are only burdened with unnecessary confusing pain and may lose availability to everyone including ourselves. Because we do care, we must join ourselves to God's will and distance ourselves from our own compulsivity and the possibly personal destructive claims others might put on us because of their overwhelming needs and fears.

In Urban Holmes' words, "*Detachment* means our freedom from being victimized by our own emotions and those to whom we minister. The opposite of detachment is not compassion, it is seduction."[7] It is through such Christian detachment that we can act out of a desire to be healthy and helpful, rather than to feel good or look good in the eyes of others. In this light, we can realize all the more why discipline is necessary for those wishing to be continually committed Christian ministers. Once again, the lesson that can save us from unnecessary pain and anxiety is: when our response to others comes out of a developed and a constantly remembered attitude of prayerful caring, we respond to the Spirit in spontaneous love, whereas when it isn't the product of such contact with the Lord in prayer, our actions may be confusing, disorganized, and eventually overwhelming to us and unresponsive to "the other" that is also Christ.

Their Pain, Our Pain

In Chekhov's words, "To a lonely man, the desert is everywhere." In moving within the desert of lonely people, the disorganized world of anxious persons, and the frightening world of both the oppressed and the hurt, we must be able to be an oasis for these people in pain. We must strive, in our attitude, not only to bring them hope and refreshment by what we do, but also to give them the more permanent, memorable relief that is only available when people feel Christ's presence as a result of who we are, i.e., people who offer a hope which is based on the promises of a resurrected Jesus.

If our hope is based only on what we can do and what we can change, in the end our efforts won't mean much to others. People have seen advanced medicine, seen good psychology, seen enlightened economics, seen Marxism, seen capitalism; some of it has helped, none has cured in a lasting way. Only God can do that; only hope founded in faith makes sense. We will only make sense as ministers to others when they see in our faces, hear in our words, and experience in our actions true hope, true prayerfulness.

When we don't come to people out of a good relationship with the Christ within, and don't move to others from the refreshing rest that comes from being with the Lord in silence and solitude, it is hard to continue to come to help; it feels "foolish" to be available with our hearts open and vulnerable. Yet, with prayer we can put aside our fears and make their pain *our* pain. We can walk with the Lord amidst the child abuse, the poverty, the emotional deprivation, the anger, and the neediness, and feel the pain without becoming confused and overwhelmed to the point of despair.

Those who see prayer as something to paste onto one's life at points in the day or at the end of the week will not be able to withstand the pain for too long. Consequently, the compassionate road will be closed or kept barely open with charity slowed down to a trickle, and the price being exacted so high that personal bitterness, skepticism, and apathy result.

For those willing to pick up the burden through "prayerful availability" the possibilities can be different, the results transformed. The road will still remain dangerous and the spiritually glib will be buried beneath it. Yet, there will be one essential difference: on each curve, on each hill, during every straight area of the road, if we are alert, if we wait with a sense of expectancy—there will be *God*. To a faith-full person, everywhere is the Lord's home.

† † †

Matthew 11:29–30

Take my yoke upon your shoulders and learn from me, for I am gentle and humble of heart. Your soul will find rest, for my yoke is easy and my burden light.

III

Being Available to . . . God

Introduction

Availability, from a Christian vantage point, can only exist in "sacred space"—that place where we can be open to the Lord. In our relationship with ourselves and others, we have seen that we can only be truly available if this space is present within us and within our community.

When the space for God is filled with self-righteousness and self-worship, we lose touch with our true selves. Without a gentle opening for God, we are filled with anger, greed, and anxiety. Likewise, when we lack the sacred space needed to make others welcome, the Spirit is shut out from giving us the love that wants to enter through a gathering of persons willing to be brothers and sisters. Thus, instead of peace, we thrive on competitiveness; we are driven by a desire for control and power. Unity is replaced with estrangement and we perceive the world as an alien place in which to live.

Availability to God in prayer radically seeks to alter such destructive movements to fill sacred space. It opens us up to the truth: the truth about ourselves, the truth about others, and the truth about God. We find that their world and our world are one when we open ourselves to God's encompassing world in prayer.

Rather than losing our true selves and cutting ourselves off from people, true prayer has a uniting influence. The following statements made by Henri Nouwen in his book *Making All Things New* and by Brother David Steindl-Rast in his recent work on *Gratefulness* emphasize this point when they speak of necessary solitude with the Lord and the topic of "genuine prayer." Nouwen writes:

> Through the discipline of solitude we discover space for God in our innermost being. Through the discipline of community we discover a place for God in our life together. Both disciplines belong together precisely because the space within us and the space among us are the same space.[1]

Steindl-Rast says,

> . . . genuine prayer comes from the heart, from that realm of my being where I am one with all. It is never a private affair. Genuine prayer is all-inclusive. A great teacher of prayer in the Jewish tradition expressed this well: "When I prepare myself to say my prayers I unite myself with all who are closer to God than I am so that, through them, I may reach God. And I also unite myself with all who may be farther away from God than I am, so that, through me, they may reach God." Christian tradition calls this the communion of saints.[2]

Creating space and opening doors to interior and interpersonal unity in Christ through prayer naturally does not occur without paying a price. In trying to be open to the gift of God's love in prayer, we need to continually try to unlearn what we have been taught which is contrary to the good news. We must work to give up the idols which temporarily deaden our burning desire for God. And we must elevate the importance of the Lord in our lives by becoming more disciplined and docile in our prayer.

Without prayer, being self-aware may indeed seem possible. Without prayer, effective social work services also may be accomplished. Yet, without prayer, without an intimate relationship with God, no space within or without will be present where we can be as fully alive and available as we are created to be. No matter who we are or what we do, the real possibilities for living are beyond us without the conversion that is nurtured by a life of prayer. No statement made here can emphasize this point strongly enough. We must take the Lord seriously through prayer. The alternative is, quite simply, a delusional uncertain form of living that continually faces us with the fact that something is missing in our hearts . . . something is very wrong in our lives.

7

Idols, Anxieties,
and Letting Go in the Dark

In a way despair is at the center of things—if only we
are prepared to go through it. We must be prepared for
a period when God is not there for us and we must be
aware of not trying to substitute a false God.

The day when God is absent, when he is silent—
that is the beginning of prayer. Not when we have a
lot to say, but when we say to God "I can't live without you; why are you so cruel, so silent?" This knowledge that we must find or die—that makes us break
through to the place where we are in the Presence. If
we listen to what our hearts know of love and longing
and are never afraid of despair, we find that victory is
always there on the other side of it.

—*Anthony Bloom*[1]

The "aha!" experience that occurs when we become an
adult is a rude, often puzzling experience, especially when we
want our relationship with God to be grown up as well. In
achieving a place in the advent of adulthood, the first realization is that we have spent the better part of our lives running
away from our insecurities. Though we may not have been
aware of it, our "pride and joy," our accomplishments, are actually covers for our negative feelings. Noteworthy achievements, while they can be good in themselves, are often the very
essence and building blocks of the "false self." With this in
mind, Merton makes the following pointed remark:

If I had a message to my contemporaries, I said, it was
surely this: be anything you like, be madmen, drunks, and

bastards of every shape and form, but at all costs avoid one thing: success.[2]

As children we recognize at an early age that the world is not the kingdom-fulfilled. From the trauma of birth through the early formative years (birth to approximately five years of age) and into the other major period of identity formation-reformation, adolescence, we see the many things that we feel are missing in ourselves. We unconsciously pick up the insecurities of our parents who, no matter how wonderful they or our early guardians were, also had issues and conflicts to confront. We begin to seek an answer to the question: Why don't I feel at peace with myself? Why am I not satisfied with myself? Why do I get upset so easily and threatened so quickly? Why don't I feel at ease with who I am and intrigued by the possibilities of who I will be as a person?

From the time our parents smile when we learn how to walk, we begin to feel we have the answer: Success! If only we can walk, then we will be fine. Then if only we can do well in school and make friends, all will be O.K. Then, if only we get into a good profession, publish a book, have a unique house, become well known . . . the stakes increase and increase. But somehow, the apparent answer (successful achievements) that we seek, and that practically everyone around us is seeking, doesn't seem to give us any sense of permanent security. Thus, we start asking ourselves the question: If I am so successful in life, how come I don't feel better? How come something is missing? Successful accomplishments, we find then, are not the criteria for achieving the solidity of adulthood; they are not the door to an open mature relationship with ourselves, others and God.

What then is the answer? If we look to the spiritual sages and the accepted current writers on the subject of leading a mature, full (holy) life which will bring with it a sense of satisfaction, the solution they offer us sounds deceivingly simple. They say, "Trust in the Lord."

Our initial response to this might be mild interest, some skepticism, and a feeling that the whole process "shouldn't be too bad." We may think, "What could it cost? How hard could it be; after all, it couldn't hurt and maybe it will make me feel nice inside. Maybe I will experience something interesting. Certainly, I can't lose anything."

At such a point we probably wouldn't make any sense of Archbishop Bloom's statement: "To meet God means to enter into the 'cave of a tiger'—it is not a pussy cat you meet—it's a tiger. The realm of God is dangerous. You must enter into it and not just seek information about it."[3]

Trust in the Lord and the surrender that this implies is actually quite difficult and elusive. Letting go of the "successful" fortress we have built up requires deep trust and subsequent significant actions in line with such a dramatic trust. Perhaps illustrations from leadership training and the field of psychotherapy would help bring this point out.

Today there are many survival courses which are offered for those wishing to test their "metal" in a physical and mental way. However, years ago leadership training programs also had brief obstacle and confidence courses which could be used to assess both physical and mental conditioning.

I remember running both courses. First came the obstacle course. It included running, climbing, and other feats involving the upper torso; being involved in it was alternately challenging, deflating, and exhilarating. Following this series of purely physical chores, another series of obstacles were set up to challenge our mental set. It was called a "confidence course." (I remember thinking after seeing some of the things they wanted us to do that it should have been called a "fear and futility course!")

There was a high tower to climb, a dark low very narrow tunnel to maneuver, and some truly intricate tasks to master. However, amidst all of these imposing challenges was what appeared to be a very foolish and basic task. It was a small ditch you had to traverse by swinging on a rope to the other side. The approach was quite simple and the goal clear; the instructors were even available to tell you how to do it. "Run up. Grab the rope. Swing over the small ditch and let go of the rope just before your feet hit the ground on the other side."

Yet, as I was watching those who tried (including some of those who had just quickly and agilely climbed a forty foot tower!), I noticed that many were failing this seemingly simple task. Some were swinging over and not letting go and swinging back; others were letting go too late and running into problems.

What seemed to be a straightforward task was proving to be difficult. The reason seemed evident. It was difficult to let go before having both feet on the ground. Yet, if you waited until both of your feet were planted while you still had the rope in your hands, it was too late. After finally letting go of the rope you would either fall back into the ditch or have to grab desperately for the rope in order to save yourself. There was only one way to succeed in dealing with this obstacle. You had to trust. You had to let go in mid-air and trust that you would land on the other side safely.

The image of this obstacle came to mind again later on in my life when as a psychotherapist I dealt with persons in treatment who had reached a point known as "working through." This is a time when persons in intensive treatment not only know intellectually what makes sense in their lives, but also begin to feel it emotionally; they are on the edge of achieving a level of insight that will lead to a new, less defensive, creative form of living.

At this stage they have rehearsed giving up unnecessary

defensive styles through their interactions with the therapist. They have seen some evidence that they can trust themselves. They are able to deal with the world in a way different than the way they dealt with people early in life. They can let down some of their inordinate psychological protective devices and give up their major destructive neurotic games. They begin to recognize that while their games and attention-getting devices produce some temporary satisfaction ("secondary gain"), they are not beneficial in the long run.

At this stage they start to feel that they can be themselves and feel that is sufficient; they don't worry that everyone will be disappointed and not love them if they express the feelings they have. But despite all of this faith and rehearsal with the therapist and some people in their lives, at the last moment they still hold back. They still are afraid of giving up their "rope," i.e., their style of dealing with the world that protected them as children, the style that is so familiar to them. They do this even though it is of little value and costs so much psychic energy today. Why?

Well, as I spoke to one patient, he described it in a way that much of the classic psychotherapy literature also bears out. He said, "If I give up some of my old ways of getting attention, and if I am not always on guard as to what people think and how I can get everyone to like me, I feel as though I'm taking a leap into the dark. The fear I have is that I won't end up on solid ground, but instead fall into an abyss. It's O.K. in here because it's as if the light is on and I can see. I think I trust you and I think I can relax and trust myself and my instincts. But when I get outside and something happens, someone frowns or doesn't give me special attention, I feel anonymous; I just can't seem to take the leap of trust and feel that I'm going to be O.K. Instead I try to be extra nice or tell people things about myself in order to manipulate them to see I'm special, I'm O.K., I'm worth something. I guess I get anxious and go back to the same old games. At least I feel safer when I play them."

What he is obviously saying is that he is almost able to let go of the rope and reach the other side—a life without the waste of energy involved in using undue defenses and protective games. However, he becomes anxious, holds onto the rope of the "devil he knows" (his old styles) and winds up back in the same spot, imprisoned by his own anxieties.

Unless confidence course runners are able to let go before their feet are firmly on the ground, they will not reach the other side of the obstacle. Unless persons in intensive psychotherapy are able to let go of old styles of protecting themselves, to trust that they are persons worthy of love and respect, and to chance not using all kinds of attention-getting devices, they will never be released from their daily turmoil; they will wake up each day and have to spend much energy trying to ensure that others like them and don't think ill of who they are or what they are doing. The same can be said of the spiritual life. When we reach the special spiritual stop in life where we are secure enough to give up competition and extreme consumption so that we can evolve as Jesus would have us, we are being asked to play by new rules, and this can cause a good deal of pressure and anxiety.

As adults we may say, "I am now ready to be more available to God. I now see that 'being' is more important than 'doing.' 'Sharing' is more spiritually sensible than 'owning.' I no longer have to run around proving myself. I no longer have to keep running ahead looking for more and more in life; it is the Lord that I want. I want to be a spiritual grown-up."

This may impact our life. We may take out time in the morning to contemplate on the words of Jesus and the letters and messages of his disciples. We may become more attuned to the Spirit during the day through a consciousness examen or thoughtful reflection of some type. We may give up trying to scheme how to make more and more money, own bigger and more expensive things, be interested in unending experiences of physical enjoyment, and in seeking merely power and personal recognition. And initially this may seem fine, may even seem peace-producing, but such rehearsal leads to the point where we must enter into greater commitment to Christ. We must let go.

We can't keep feet in both worlds. Possibly we have noticed that while we are being drawn to be more and more spiritual, give up more and more of our old ways, there is a fear of remaining faithful to the spiritual life. We begin to recognize that we really somehow hoped to be both the old person and the new person.

Conflict is present. On the one hand, our readings and reflections are calling us to be more available to God by being disciplined in our prayer time and being more concerned how to be like Jesus; on the other hand, we are becoming anxious that life is passing us by, that we are deluding ourselves about a God that doesn't exist while others who care less about God seem to be enjoying themselves.

Karl Rahner reflects:

> Look at the vast majority of men, Lord—and excuse me if I presume to pass judgment on them—but do they often think of You? Are You the First Beginning and Last End for them, the One without whom their minds and hearts can find no rest? Don't they manage to get along perfectly well without You? Don't they feel quite at home in this world which they know so well, where they can be sure of just what they have to reckon with? Are You anything more for them than the One who sees to it that the world stays on its hinges, so they won't have to call on You?[4]

In this statement, he is complaining about his state of faith, his position as someone who has been called to give up the old and put on the new. He is in this stage of adult faith (and adult conflict) and crying out, "Why have You burnt Your mark in my soul in Baptism?"[5] "Why have You made me feel unfulfilled without You?" Such turmoil unfortunately is not the only problem.

As well as anxiety that the joy of living is passing us by, *boredom* is another experience we must deal with when we commit ourselves to growing up spiritually. When we stop competing for a place in the world's sun and start letting go of the compulsively formed false self, we recognize how addicted we are to trying to fill our life with any kind of meaning which the secular world says is important (fame, wealth, power). We begin to recognize that the quest for God is something that has to be developed just as the quest for being a "god" of a false kingdom was. My work with drug addicts helps me see this in myself and others.

In working with an addict who was detoxified and desirous of leading a productive, drug-free life, a question came up as to what he would do with his free time. We were talking about the need he had not only to find a job and a place to live but also to have outlets so he would not be tempted to turn back to drugs, and he said, "But what would I do in my spare time?" I said, "Well, what did you do before?" "Nothing. I was too busy. You see when I wasn't high, I was concerned about how I was going to get the $150 each day to pay for my drugs. Then, when I got the money together I had to find the guy with the stuff. Then I took the stuff. Then I was high. Then I was worried because I was coming down. Then I needed to get money again. The whole thing took a lot of time—all my time!"

With this, he looked at me for guidance to what he could do for fun now that he wasn't consumed with the search for drugs. Much to my surprise, I couldn't think of a thing. (I knew I was in trouble because the only thing that came to mind was bowling!)

I began to recognize that this addict had to learn to play in a healthy way again. Like a child he had to begin to develop a taste for the healthy life again. With the right attitude, patience, and discipline, he would have to begin awkwardly to try life out anew.

The same thing must happen for us. We must become like little children again if we are to give up old idols, face our anxieties, and let go in the dark. Just as the addict felt foolish when he began to try to enjoy conversation about things other than drugs, go to a movie or a museum, and become high on life rather than passively move to a stuperous, slow self-destruction, we will also have to undergo awkward learning periods. In the words of one of the "Desert Mothers" (Amma Syncletica), "In the beginning, there is struggle and a lot of work for those who come near to God. But after that, there is indescribable joy. It is just like building a fire: at first it's smoky and your eyes water, but later you get the desired results. Thus we ought to light the divine fire in ourselves with tears and effort."[6]

In doing this, we must also be careful not to submit to the temptation to run away from the dark journey to God. Replacing God seems so easy and so tempting. We can begin to search again for a bigger house, nicer friends, a better work assignment, a vacation home, a special car or possession. We can seek the answer in an attempt to replay life with a new younger partner if we are married, or a unique following if we are a religious leader. We can find a consuming hobby or apostolate, or turn to alcohol as a special warm, glowing friend.

The temptation to turn away from God and to ourselves is great. Finley notes in his book on the ideas of Merton: "In our zeal to become the landlords of our own being we cling to

each achievement as a kind of verification of our self-pro-
claimed reality. We become the center and God somehow re-
cedes to an invisible fringe."[7] But none of these will last. None
can replace God. Charles de Foucauld was quoted as saying in
the book *The Sands of Tamanrasset*, ". . . when you leave the
world to give yourself to God, there is no return."[8] Once we
recognize that only God can alleviate our deep yearning for satisfaction we can never completely fool ourselves again.

As adults who have tried to understand ourselves, be open
to others and be more available to God, there is no choice but
to go on if we are to be satisfied. If we turn around, we will be
as unhappy as the young man who came to Jesus to ask what
more he could do in his quest for holiness. The fact that you
are reading this book and I am writing it means that we are out
in the open. We already see the need; we already agree with
the necessity of the quest for Christ. Rahner puts it so beautifully:

> For a Christian, his Christian existence is ultimately the
> totality of his existence. This totality opens out into the
> dark abysses of the wilderness which we call God. When
> one undertakes something like this, he stands before the
> great thinkers, the saints, and finally Jesus Christ. The
> abyss of existence opens up in front of him. He knows that
> he has not thought enough, has not loved enough, and has
> not suffered enough.[9]

Once we have opened our eyes, we can no longer shut them
tightly enough to blind ourselves to the goal for which every
human being was created: to experience the Lord. If we can
begin to accept this fact, the cost, be it great or small, will start
to become irrelevant and the journey to God will be the only
thing worthy of focus.

† † †

John 14: 15–18

If you love me and obey the commands I give you, I will ask the Father and he will give you another Paraclete—to be with you always: the Spirit of truth, whom the world cannot accept since it neither sees him nor recognizes him; but you can recognize him because he remains with you and will be within you. I will not leave you orphaned; I will come back to you.

8

Experiencing the Lord

> In a secular society such as our own, where we are taught *not* to expect to experience God, it is particularly important that those who serve God cultivate an intentional model of prayer that breaks through the hard crust of the surface memory to the deeper self, which is relatively untouched by the collective representations of our environment.
>
> —*Urban Holmes III*[1]

Experiencing the Lord is a goal in life; as a matter of fact, it is the only goal. This may not be appreciated now since inadvertently we may have been indoctrinated to relegate God to church and the mountain top. As we know, this hasn't always been the case. In poetic literature, the Bible, and earlier works, God was seen everywhere. One of the marvelous gripping elements of the Old Testament is the presence of God. Each page ripples with an awareness of the Lord.

The New Testament carries this sensitivity a step further, especially in John's Gospel and Epistles. The Spirit is felt, and we don't feel orphaned as we experience God among us in the love and thrill of early community experiences in the Church. Before and after the Old and New Testaments were written, God also was felt in oral and written poetry. People looked at the earth, the sea and the sky and they saw God. We have lost much of this. Now, for us, the land is something to be owned, the sea something to be polluted, and the sky a place to put new weapons.

How can we get back in touch with God? How can we

begin to find the Lord again in the environment, in the people we live with, in ourselves? How can we unify the world again in the Spirit of the Lord Jesus so that nothing is left out, so that all is transformed?

Although there are no easy answers to these questions, there are certainly available approaches if we are willing to take them. Yet, whichever one we take, the enemies of our desire to be available to God in a profound, pervasive way must be faced. Prominent among such forces within us and the world are: (1) the distractions from, and discouragement against, being spiritual (in relationship with the Lord), and (2) the natural tendency which is encouraged in many corners to be fragmented and live in a very compartmentalized way. To deal with such divisive trends, an appreciation of the need for solitude with God and the nurturance of a relationship with the Lord that brings us to a greater appreciation of creation are essential.

Distractions and Discouragement

Distractions are the result of the spiritual friction we feel and the psychological static we hear when we try to turn to God in solitude and silence. Distraction is not really the problem in this instance; discouragement is. If we let ourselves get discouraged, the danger of abandoning the search altogether becomes more of an ominous possibility. One way of deflating such feelings of defeat is by understanding some of the types of distractions and by reflecting on some of the ways to deal with them and our occasionally unrealistic expectations about a life of prayer.

The types of distractions which concern us most here are distractions *from* prayer and distractions *within* prayer. Distractions from prayer are common because we are an action-oriented society which likes to encourage self-worship. Since we are from a culture that values "doing," even the most spiritually committed among us have to constantly deal with a gnawing belief that prayer is not as important as action. Consequently, if anything has to drop out of our schedule it is prayer time.

Part of the reason for this is also our belief that prayer is like a mini-escape or vacation. We only run to it when work is done or we need a respite from our pressures. Is it any wonder then that we don't value the time for prayer as an encounter with the Lord in solitude but see it instead as a self-indulgent time for which we feel guilty, given our busy schedule. Given such an outlook on prayer, is it any wonder that we fail to be as alert when we do turn ourselves in solitude to God?

Distractions from prayer also include the ones we have from being "prayerful." Just as we are influenced not to be centered on the Lord through a daily period of solitude, we also are indoctrinated to separate the sacred and the secular. Such a negative influence goes directly against Teilhard de Chardin and others (e.g., Matthew Fox) whose influence in modern times is to encourage us to embrace *all* things as sacred signs of God.

This movement away from seeing God in all things is steeped in our desire to deny our dependence upon God and to join with each other in building a communal false self designed to set its own standards, give its own rewards, and worship itself. Merton often took pains to point this out to us. In his own words,

> The mother of all lies is the lie we persist in telling ourselves about ourselves. And since we are not brazen enough liars to make ourselves believe our own lie individually, we pool all our lies together and believe them be-

cause they have become the big lie uttered by the *vox populi*, and this kind of lie we accept as ultimate truth.[2]

Yet, despite this lie, the truth still manages to seep through. Whether I'm lecturing to a group of people interested in self-awareness, or sitting with a person in therapy, or walking down the street with a friend, I find that the conversation often turns to the same feeling: *something's missing*. People are thirsting for something deep. There is a hunger for something truly meaningful.

J.-P. Dubois-Dumée noted this point quite well in a paper he wrote on renewal of prayer:

In this spiritual renewal, I believe that one can detect among other things:

a need for permanence in a civilization of transience;
a need for the Absolute when all else is becoming relative;
a need for silence in the midst of noise;
a need for gratuitousness in the face of unbelievable greed;
a need for poverty amid the flaunting of wealth;
a need for contemplation in a century of action, for without contemplation, action risks becoming mere agitation;
a need for communication in a universe content with entertainment and sensationalism;
a need for peace amid today's universal outbursts of violence;
a need for quality to counterbalance the increasingly prevalent response to quantity;
a need for humility to counteract the arrogance of power and science;

a need for human warmth when everything is being rationalized or computerized;

a need to belong to a small group rather than to be part of the crowd;

a need for slowness to compensate the present eagerness for speed;

a need for truth when the real meaning of words is distorted in political speeches and sometimes even in religious discourses;

a need for transparency when everything seems opaque.

Yes, a need for the interior life . . .[3]

Consequently, we must reach out and grasp the stark truth reflected in this need and hold on tightly to the need to pray and be prayerful. The interior life, and the view that sees creation and God as one, go hand in hand. To be dissuaded from either vision of God is to submit to something less than God, something that isn't true.

Distractions *within* prayer also keep us from concentrating on the Lord with love. (By "prayer" I'm referring here to those contemplative periods where we are alone with the Lord.) If they are comprised of a lot of little things, taking the suggestion of the author of the classic, *The Cloud of Unknowing*, might be of help. He suggests that we look around them or over them, so to speak, as a way of refocusing on God again. Another widespread approach is the use of the "Jesus Prayer." In this instance we silently utter the name of Jesus in our hearts as a way of quieting down and centering ourselves on God.

There are times though when certain distractions repeat themselves and seem to demand center stage. A friend might be sick, we may have financial problems, there may be an issue we have with alcohol abuse, there may be someone who frightens us or with whom we are angry, or we may have sexual feelings which bother us. In these instances, many people experienced in spiritual direction suggest to us that we shouldn't try to go around or ignore these interruptions, but see them as parts of our life that need to be integrated in the Lord. So, instead of fighting them, we present them to the Lord for healing attention. In laying them to rest in the Lord, we can then concentrate on God instead of ourselves and our problems.

Maybe we won't be as successful as we like. (Usually I'm not.) However, we probably should take care not to expect too much or try to achieve contemplation on our own. After all, although we can be disciplined as a way of trying to take the Lord seriously, a relationship with God is a *gift*. We can be open to it, but we don't have the power in ourselves to achieve it. Rather than working hard at prayer, staying faithful to a continual surrender to the will of God seems really more in line with the openness we should emulate. Once again in the words of Finley on the spirituality of Merton:

> One cannot force the issue here. A forced determined effort to continue praying in the face of adversity, dryness, and emptiness may be nothing but the false self attempting to prove its endurance. There must rather be but a simple desire for God and a humble detachment from experiences or the lack of experiences. Merton once told me that "in silent prayer we must simply realize that we are in water over our head." In these waters the false self quickly panics and heads for shore. But the true self, secure in its humility, finds these waters to be a womb from which, in an unexpected eternal moment, it is brought forth by him who makes all things new.
>
> And so asking how to realize the true self is much like facing a large field covered with snow that has not yet been walked on and asking, "Where is the path?" The answer is to walk across it and there will be a path.[4]

A Fragmented Self, A Compartmentalized World

Prayer is a unifying force. As with any powerful drive, even though it is based on love, it is threatening because it challenges us to change, to mature, to evolve as persons. Being united within requires a surrender of our desires to hold onto the status quo at all cost, and a willingness to enter into a more open dependent relationship with the Lord. Since this entails the facing of our own games (so the hurt and fears that encourage their continuance can be healed in the presence of the Lord), there is a natural resistance to the unity that comes from being really honest. Giving up familiar approaches, even if they are really not in our best interest, can be a very anxiety-producing occurrence.

Denying, suppressing, rationalizing our actions, and projecting the blame elsewhere is sometimes such a reflex action that honesty and openness are not easy. For instance, in trying to look at something unpleasant we did or felt, we normally feel embarrassed and want to avoid it. No one has to be present with us. No one has to know what we are thinking, but still we are embarrassed when we look at something which is contrary to the image of ourselves that we have tried to project to everyone—including ourselves and God. Fragmentation within serves to keep the truth from us most of the time. In that way we don't have to feel anxious about our faults and we sometimes doubt our utter dependence on a God who exists in a world where we're taught that the only actual movement depends on human action. Yet, the price of our denials and falsehoods in the long run is high, and the presentation of our unspecific, lukewarm, sweeping ventilations of our sinfulness is actually a subtle evasion of accepting the truth about ourselves.

The author Trevanian in one of his novels wrote, "Confession is good for the spirit . . . it empties the soul, making more space for sin."[5] When we fail to candidly and clearly admit our thoughts, feelings and behaviors without all of the "psychological dressing," nothing is seen for what it is; nothing changes in us. Still, maybe that's what we want; at least, maybe that's what the anxious part of us wants. In our heart we know that we can ask the Lord for healing. However, at some level we want it to come as magic, not in the form of Jesus standing with us so we can face our fears with his help.

The reality is that we can learn to let go of the hurt. We can take action to curb such impulses as excessive use of alcohol or food. We can deal with our anger so that it is understood and channeled appropriately. And we can be willing to take responsibility for ourselves and all our actions. God will help us if we turn to him and sit in solitude and seriously ask for courage. There is an old Talmudic story that says the sea did not divide when Moses put the rod over it *until* the first person took a step into the water. We will not be refused the gentle healing of Jesus, but for our part we must also respond by trusting God and acting accordingly.

External compartmentalization also encourages inner fragmentation. Rather than seeing ourselves as always being in the presence of God, we usually see ourselves as working, playing, praying, and so forth. The result of this is that we begin to divide our lives, ignore people and events, live for the weekends, and specialize our existence to the point where we have lost touch with the primary thread of our own life, our sense of meaning and purpose.

Such division of things ironically causes us to prioritize things incorrectly. We see a report as essential, and talking to a child, even if he or she is our own child, as a wasted intrusion. We concentrate on all the good we'd like to do for the world when we give a talk or volunteer our time at some event, but ignore the special possibilities that a brief meeting with an elderly neighbor acquaintance or fellow community member has to offer.

From the time we get up, the morning news shows tell what they believe is important as well as whom they feel we should "worship." Therefore, unless we pray and allow the Lord to form us and unless we consciously prepare ourselves graciously each day to meet all who come to us, we will begin to treat people based on such images and illusions. In this light then, prayer is not a place to merely sit back and let our mind wander on irrelevancies. It is a place to face ourselves and the world. It is a place to relax in the peace and security of the Lord, yes; but it is also a place to be alert and open to what God wants, not what the status quo within us and society desire. This is the "tiger in the cave" that Archbishop Bloom talks about, not the kind of Jesus that we sometimes like to form in our own minds.

"Alone" with the Lord in Solitude

If we carry a compartmentalized view of the world with us into our period of solitude with the Lord and try to relax and open our hearts to the Spirit, we will be in for a surprise. Although we may be sitting quietly in an empty room, we will realize that if we are truly being prayerful we are not alone with the Lord, but we are with the whole spectrum of our friends, relatives, and those we don't even know. When we greet the Lord in solitude, we bring the world with us.

First, others are there as a source of distraction. They are like tiny gnats keeping us from focusing on God. Then others are there as a "wonderful" source of escape. They fill our time so that we don't have to face our own nothingness and our own fears that we are deluding ourselves and that God in fact doesn't really exist. Finally, they are there as *Christ*. No longer are they interfering or alien forces; at this point we have the opportunity to be one with them—in their sorrows and joys—in the Spirit.

How does this all happen? Not easily, not through our own efforts, and certainly not with the help of a secular philosophy of how to live in the world. In terms of the practical, dollar-and-cents, accomplishment-oriented, self-made-person world, praying is stupid. And that's how we feel much of the time when we begin our efforts at solitude with the Lord. (Also, such feelings occasionally return vividly and convincingly to some of us even after our prayer life is, to our mind, quite developed.) Yet all is possible with the Lord.

Spending time quietly with the Lord is a good way to approach God. There are many ways to do this and many good books to serve as a guide. (See "Selected Bibliography on Prayer" at the end of this book.) Primarily, though, the basics are straightforward. We simply take out some time each day to sit quietly with the Lord. As St. John of the Cross says, "The language that God hears best is the silent language of love."

We can begin with a prayer or a few lines of Scripture. Then we just sit and quietly spend time with the Lord. In the beginning we may talk to God and, hearing "nothing," feel that the time is frustrating and useless. As we start, we may look for a mystical experience, and in turn miss the Lord's "voice." Or, we may struggle with distractions and after twenty minutes think to ourselves, "I'll bet I spent one moment concentrating on the Lord, the rest thinking about everything else under the sun," whereas the actual reality might have been that we spent twenty minutes with the Lord but only remembered one.

Still, if we continue to stay with the Lord and continue to ask seriously for Jesus to send the Spirit, all will be fine. Discouragement is a natural demon; doubts are expected experiences in the fabric of prayer. With love, trust in the Lord, and patience, availability to God and God's availability to us will open like a warm meadow in front of us. Our eyes will then be able to see things in the way God meant them to be.

Henri Nouwen puts it beautifully when he says, "Solitude is the furnace in which . . . transformation takes place."[6] Quietly as we sit with the Lord, then, we may begin to experience life anew. Prior to this, we might be like Nicodemus wondering how we could be born again; with prayer though, our eyes may be opened to see the world in wonder as little children do.

In such instances as this, we give up the puny passions that are molded by the world of competition and possession. Instead, in our surrender to God in solitude they are replaced with the gentle passions of gratefulness, wonder, and acceptance. But we cannot make it happen; we can only ask for the gift—the gift that comes in our relationship with the Lord.

Relationship with the Lord

Knowing *about* someone is completely different from actually knowing someone. In the former instance the quality of the relationship is distance. Even close physical proximity doesn't bridge the gap. The fact still remains that the person is a stranger. Intimacy is only possible when we actually know someone, when we have gone through the anxieties, the games, the personal doubts, the superficiality of it all. This point is a particularly poignant one when speaking about prayer.

Richard Hauser, in his book *In His Spirit*, makes this issue clear when he says, "Since prayer is the expression of our relationship with God, it will always reflect the quality of this relationship . . . if we want to improve our prayer, we must first improve our relationship."[7] There are many ways to improve our relationship with someone. Probably the most basic is to take the effort to know someone and to allow this person to know us. In other words, we must move from the stage of "knowing about" to "intimacy."

This takes time, patience, and willingness. To know God there must be a willingness to give time to the relationship. As in a serious relationship this must not be the "left-over" time; it needs to be important time, scheduled time. Then in this time there must be patience and a willingness to listen. If we meet someone and take all of the time talking about ourselves, our needs, and our impressions of the other person, we will never get to know the individual. Instead we will appear to be saying to him or her that we actually want to avoid intimacy; we don't care to know the person; we are only interested in ourselves. Or, in a deeper sense, we are saying that we are afraid of intimacy. We are afraid of the demands that might be made, the truths that might be uttered, the expectations the person might have of us. The same can be said about our relationship with the Lord.

When we play at prayer, rather than open ourselves up to listen, it is we who are truly not available to God. Accordingly, when we are not willing to pay the price of intimacy by being "fools for Christ" in the eyes of the world, what can we expect from God? This is the question we must face. This is the question we must reflect on. The answer to it is obviously not in the heavens or in any book. The answer is found in our heart.

✝   ✝   ✝

Romans 13:2

Do not conform yourselves to this age but be transformed by the renewal of your mind, so that you may judge what is God's will, what is good, pleasing and perfect.

In the Presence of God: An Epilogue

> To pray, I think, does not mean to think about God
> in contrast to thinking about other things, or to spend
> time with God instead of spending time with other
> people. Rather, it means to think and live in the pres-
> ence of God. As soon as we begin to divide our
> thoughts into thoughts about God and thoughts about
> people and events, we remove God from our daily life
> and put him in a pious little niche where we can think
> pious thoughts and experience pious feelings. Al-
> though it is important and even indispensable for the
> spiritual life to set apart time for God and God alone,
> prayer can only become unceasing prayer when all our
> thoughts—beautiful or ugly, high or low, proud or
> shameful, sorrowful or joyful—can be thought in the
> presence of God.
>
> —*Henri J.M. Nouwen*[1]

"True availability" is born and grows only in the presence
of the Lord. It is a "gestalt" that can't be divided. Being available just to ourselves, only to others, or solely to a transcendent
God is not real availability; it is merely an artificial compartmentalized form of attentiveness. The danger in trying to emphasize one area of life to the detriment or denial of the other
is tantamount to replacing God, the encompassing Light, with
an imitation of our own or another's invention.

Renoir's reaction to the modernization of his church's altar
lighting was, "What riches! To think how the priests have re-

placed that living light by the dead light of electricity. . . . It is bottled light only fit for corpses."[2] This is the kind of dramatic reaction we should have on a greater scale when we are asked to replace our own vital spiritual philosophy of living with a lesser, more mechanical and fragmented one.

Emphasizing only "the self" leads to a self-preoccupation that distorts reality and sets the stage for narcissism and moodiness. In losing interest in others and thinking only of ourselves there is a risk of experiencing grandiosity in both positive and negative directions. In being very self-centered, any event that happens to us, or any fears we may have, become greatly magnified; everything becomes distorted through the repulsive magnifying glass of self-absorption and self-protection.

In such cases, so great may be our anxieties that we may even seek to avoid any reflective periods at all. The belief may be, "I think too much. I worry about everything. It's too upsetting. The hell with it!" Avoidance of self-reflection, however, is obviously not the answer to self-absorption. Anthony Bloom illustrates this well when he points to the consequences of a lack of a prayerful reflectiveness in his book *Beginning To Pray*:

> There is a passage in Dickens' *Pickwick Papers* which is a very good description of my life and probably of your lives. Pickwick goes to the club. He hires a cab and on the way he asks innumerable questions. Among the questions, he says "Tell me, how is it possible that such a mean and miserable horse can drive such a big and heavy cab?" The cabbie replies "It's not a question of the horse, Sir, it's a question of the wheels," and Mr. Pickwick says "What do you mean?" The cabbie answers "You see, we have a magnificent pair of wheels which are so well oiled that it is enough for the horse to stir a little for the wheels to begin to turn and then the poor horse must run for its life." Take the way in which we live most of the time. We are not the

horse that pulls, we are the horse that runs away from the
cab in fear of its life. [3]

We must try to be self-aware if we are not to live our lives
as bowling balls caught in a slippery gutter. But this needs to
be done in light of the Gospel, in light of our relationship with
others, and constantly in the presence of God. Mere compartmentalized introspection needs to be replaced, therefore, by a
unifying *Christian* form of introspection.

Christian introspection is not merely discovering the positive and negative self. Instead, it is a prayerful process of dis-
covery in which we search for the ways in which we have
closed the doors to God's presence. The goal, then, is not self-
worship but continual change in our self-definition, to bring it
in line with an openness to Christ. It is this openness that is a
response to Christ's claim on us. The "push" behind self-anal-
ysis is us; the push behind Christian introspection is God.

As we search and counsel ourselves pastorally, the goal is
not the avoidance of necessary pain. It is not the deification of
self. It is not an abrogation of the responsibility to serve and
be interested in others. Rather, it is a search to see how we can
be strengthened and comforted by God in our goal to make life
meaningful for ourselves and others. In this sense, only *unnecessary* masochistic pain is avoided; the suffering that comes with
living a life full of the Spirit is accepted. [4]

With an effort at becoming involved in Christian self-
awareness we seek not to punish ourselves for our shortcom-
ings or praise ourselves for our talents; we merely seek the
truth about ourselves. In a sense we try to become "small"—
small enough to see the Lord in ourselves, small enough to see
Jesus in others, and small enough to hear his word in solitude
(1 Kings 19:12). This quality of "smallness" that we need is the
result of part of our quest to seek the crystal truth about ourselves; it is designed to deflate any grandiosity and self-infla-

tion which clouds our personal vision. But, in the process, we must ensure that our efforts to become small do not represent a form of retreat from the world.

Schizophrenics sometimes make their world smaller because they are anxious about their own emotional vulnerability. A pioneer of Rorschach (ink blot) test interpretation, Zygmunt Piotrowski, used to refer to such psychotic individuals as "*alpha* schizophrenics." They made their world smaller so they would have less to contend with in life. They could then feel safer and more able to cope.

Yet, for us, in becoming smaller as a response to the Spirit, security and retreat are not the goals. Perspective and strength are the goals by which we become less filled with ourselves, less apt to burst at the least negative comment from another person and less apt to blow up after seeing our personal failures for what they really are. Instead, as we become more humble we actually are able and willing to risk more and move out amidst those who need the gentle touch of Jesus—the touch that can be felt when we are truly compassionate in his name, rather than in the name of our own need to be loved and recognized.

When we meet others interpersonally merely to do good or to be seen as good, the healing possibilities are limited. They are limited to the physical actions we take and the time frame in which we take them. But true availability to others recognizes a greater value, a more important purpose. It is this greater value and purpose that the world really needs to experience in us. Kenneth Leech notes in his book *True Prayer:*

> To recognize holiness is to recognize the activity of God in
> people. More than that, holiness manifests the character,
> the nature of God. . . . Holiness never points to itself but
> always beyond itself to God. The saint is essentially some-

one who communicates and radiates the character of God, his love, his joy, his peace. . . . And the world needs saints, Simone Weil wrote, just as a plague-stricken city needs doctors.[5]

Christian self-awareness, by definition, needs to be joined somehow to Christian relationship with, and real compassion for, others. These two go hand-in-hand; they are firmly bonded together in solidarity when, in silence and solitude, we place ourselves in the presence of God.

Prayerful solitude with God makes it possible for us to be with others and to deal intimately even with those in pain. The reason is not that our time quietly spent with the Lord helps us to be *above* the pain. Instead, it allows us to be detached from being totally overwhelmed by the consequences of the pain by maintaining a hope based on a faith carried within. So, even when we seemingly have no peace, there is still something strong within that gives direction and clarity; we feel at some level that there is a way beyond all the hurt. We seem to appreciate both that God is here now and yet naturally yearn for more of the Lord's greater transforming presence (Romans 8:21).

Also, in solitude with the Lord our sense of self-awareness and sense of personal asceticism can become clearer. We don't have to become compulsively preoccupied with our tendencies and impulses; prayer of its very nature can instruct us on how to deal with such subtle movements in our lives. In the words of the unknown fourteenth century author of *The Cloud of Unknowing*, "If you give yourself generously to the work of love, I feel sure you will know when to begin and end every other activity. I cannot believe that a person wholeheartedly given to contemplation will err by excess or default in these external matters—unless he is a person who is always wrong . . . it is better to achieve moderation in these things through heedless-ness than through anxious introspection, as if this would help determine the appropriate measure."[6]

Prayer helps then to maintain clarity. It encourages us to see ourselves for who we are, as well as to be happy with the dependence we have on God. It helps us to see the attitude of compassion for what it is, and avoid the pitfalls inherent in helping others for what we can get out of it rather than for the gentle experience it can produce in others and ourselves. Fi-nally, prayer can help us resist imaging idols rather than God and making more of the joys of life than we ought.

Bloom clearly noted a number of years ago: "As long as our imagination has not taken hold of us, things are outside of us; once our imagination has got entangled and imprisoned in things, then we are glued to things. . . . If you settle down and ask yourself 'I'm not really hungry but there are so many nice things one can eat, what would I fancy?' in five minutes you will have projected tentacles over a variety of things. . . . To begin with say 'no.' If you haven't said 'no' in time, you are in for a fight. But then be ruthless about it, because reason and detachment is more precious than what you get as a slave in terms of enjoyment."[7]

And so, if there is a key to understanding the problems of availability and appreciating it as a gift, this key is contained in our seeking *unity* within and without by placing ourselves continually in the presence of God: to relax, to sit, to learn, to work, to contemplate, to do everything in the presence of God. Yet, care must be taken not to envision ourselves in the pres-ence of a *superego* (conscience)-oriented childhood deity who we might have felt was always looking over our shoulder ensuring we didn't do anything wrong, but instead we must place our-selves before an *ego* (reality)-oriented, loving God who is trying to help us as adults to image the world as a place where the gentle presence of the Lord is both needed and possible.

Availability is a great gift; it is a gift to behold, a gift to cherish, a gift to share. Yet, as in any living gift, availability must be nurtured if it is to thrive and be a continual source of joy. The challenge is knowing how and when to do this; and the satisfaction is in knowing that if we continually try to be open to God, we will never lose it.

Selected Bibliography on Prayer

There are many excellent books on prayer. The following brief, annotated list was developed with an eye to the theme of this book. It contains a sampling of readable contemporary works which can serve to introduce the topics of prayer to ourselves or—in the case of the spiritual director—those whom we guide.

Prayer

Bloom, Anthony. *Beginning To Pray*. Ramsey, New Jersey: Paulist, 1970.

This modern classic is written for people who have never prayed before; however, it is a joy to read no matter what level of spiritual development the person may be at. Its simple, stark prose makes one realize that the author is writing from experience, not merely from theory.

Faricy, Robert and Wicks, Robert. *Contemplating Jesus*. Mahwah, New Jersey: Paulist, 1986.

This very compact book on contemplation is based on two addresses given at Neumann College by Robert Faricy, S.J. Working with him to integrate the material was a joy! I am pleased that the resulting short work is filled with clear, practical information which should prove useful to people interested in contemplation and those directors who guide them.

Hauser, Richard J. *In His Spirit: A Guide to Today's Spirituality.* Ramsey, New Jersey: Paulist, 1982.

A very basic book which presents a practical introduction to some key current themes in spirituality. His concrete examples and illustrations, as well as the informal style, make this a very readable book.

Nouwen, Henri J.M. *Making All Things New: An Invitation to the Spiritual Life.* San Francisco: Harper and Row, 1981.

This is a small, simple and beautiful discussion of the "spiritual life." It helps the reader cut through life's entangling preoccupations to see the unifying presence of God in our lives.

Nouwen, Henri J.M. *The Way of the Heart: Desert Spirituality and Contemporary Ministry.* New York: Seabury, 1981.

This book is one of the most deeply prayerful ones I have ever read. It brings the words of the desert fathers and mothers to life in a way that helps people to approach God in silence and solitude so as to be less prone to being overcome by the compulsions of the world. In this book, Henri Nouwen has given a very special gift to everyone interested in being alive with the Lord.

Prayerfulness

Fox, Matthew. *On Becoming a Musical Mystical Bear: Spirituality American Style.* Ramsey, New Jersey: Paulist, 1972.

This is one of Matthew Fox's earlier spirited and polemic works on spirituality. It is a good book to help one break out of stereotypical responses to God in life. Written with a flare it encourages people to respond to life fully and openly.

McNeill, Donald P., Morrison, Douglas A., and Nouwen, Henri, J.M. *Compassion.* New York: Doubleday, 1982.

This book is designed to help people to see the necessity of opening up to finding Christ in the world, in other people—especially the financially poor, the emotionally depressed, and the politically oppressed. Yet, this book doesn't approach the topic in a naively romantic manner. Instead it asks people both to unmask their unrealistic expectations and to nurture a Christian hope based on a strong faith and reflected in a concrete demonstration of charity.

Steindl-Rast, David. *Gratefulness, the Heart of Prayer: An Approach to Life in Fullness.* Ramsey, New Jersey: Paulist, 1984.

This delightful book enables the reader to see how easy it is to limit our acceptance of, and gratitude for, life. The tendency in most people is to leave the house each morning with a list. On it are those things one would be grateful for (e.g., wealth, success, power, recognition). David Steindl-Rast in his book Gratefulness *encourages all to throw away their lists and start each day looking for the surprise that comes with being open to Christ in a new way, even in the previously familiar parts of life.*

Notes

1. UNIQUENESS

1. Martin Buber, *Way of Man*, New York: Lyle Stuart, 1966, Chapter One.
2. J.A. Sanford, *Healing and Wholeness*, New York: Paulist Press, 1977, p. 16.

2. FAILURE AND FORGIVENESS

1. Lawrence Sanders, *The Case of Lucy Bending*, New York: Putnam/Berkley Edition, 1982, p. 42.
2. J. Edelwich and A. Brodsky, *Burnout: Stages of Disillusionment in the Helping Professions*, New York: Human Science Press, 1980; H. Freudenberger, *Burnout*, New York: Anchor/Doubleday, 1980; J.J. Gill, "Burnout: A Growing Threat in the Ministry," *Human Development*, 1(2) Summer 1980, pp. 21–27; C. Maslach, "Burned-Out," *Human Behavior*, September 1976; W. Schafer, *Stress, Distress, and Growth*, Davis, California: Responsible Action, 1978.
3. Jurgen Moltmann, *Theology of Hope*, New York: Harper and Row, 1967.
4. R. Wicks, *Christian Introspection: Self-Ministry Through Self-Understanding*, New York: Crossroad, 1983.
5. J.T. Carmody and D.L. Carmody, *Contemporary Catholic Theology: An Introduction*, San Francisco: Harper and Row, 1980, p. 9.

3. SELF-AWARENESS

1. Henry David Thoreau, quoted by W.H. Auden in his Introduction to Dag Hammarskjold's *Markings*, New York: Knopf, 1976, p. ix.
2. K. Leech, *True Prayer*, New York: Harper and Row, 1980, pp. 43–44.

3. J. LeCarré, *The Little Drummer Girl*, New York: Knopf, 1983, p. 365.

4. R. Wicks, *Christian Introspection: Self-Ministry Through Self-Understanding*, New York: Crossroad, 1983, p. 110.

4. CLARITY

1. M. Scott Peck, "Self-Ministry," *Ministries*, April 1980, p. 7.

2. Henri J. Nouwen, *The Genesee Diary*, New York: Doubleday (Image Edition), 1981, p. 108.

3. *Ibid.*, p. 119.

4. Henri J.M. Nouwen, *Making All Things New*, New York: Harper and Row, 1981, p. 25.

5. Anthony Bloom, *Beginning To Pray*, Ramsey: Paulist Press, 1970, p. 45.

6. David Steindl-Rast, *Gratefulness*, Ramsey: Paulist Press, 1984, p. 142.

7. *Ibid.*, p. 89.

8. Henri J.M. Nouwen, *The Genesee Diary*, New York: Doubleday (Image Edition), 1981, p. 81.

9. James Finley, *Merton's Palace of Nowhere: A Search for God Through Awareness of the True Self*, Notre Dame: Ave Maria, 1978, p. 76.

10. Karl Rahner, *Encounters with Silence*, Westminster: Newman Press, 1960, p. 5.

5. RELATIONSHIPS

1. Karl Rahner, *Foundations of Christian Faith*, N.Y.: Crossroad, 1978, p. 74.

2. W.H. Auden, "Introduction" to Dag Hammarskjold's *Markings*, N.Y.: Knopf, 1976, p. ix.

3. Henri J.M. Nouwen, *The Genesee Diary*, N.Y.: Doubleday, 1976 (Image Edition, 1981), p. 84.

4. Thomas Hora, "Existentialism and Psychiatry: The Transpersonal Perspective," Comments made at the "Round Table on Ex-

istentialism and Psychiatry" presented at the Annual Meeting of the American Psychiatric Association in Toronto, Canada on May 8, 1962.

6. THEIR PAIN, OUR FEARS

1. Jack Nelson, *Hunger for Justice*, Maryknoll: Orbis, 1980, p. vii.

2. Statement by Albert Schweitzer cited in Gilbert Hay, *This Way to Happiness*, New York: Simon and Schuster, 1967, p. 35.

3. Donald P. McNeill, Douglas A. Morrison, and Henri J.M. Nouwen, *Compassion*, New York: Doubleday, 1982.

4. Robert Faricy, *Praying for Inner Healing*, London: SCM, 1979, p. 40.

5. David Steindl-Rast, *Gratefulness, the Heart of Prayer*, Ramsey: Paulist Press, 1984, p. 200.

6. James Whitehead, "An Asceticism of Time," *Review for Religious 39*, 1980, p. 3.

7. Urban Holmes, *Spirituality for Ministry*, San Francisco: Harper & Row, 1982, p. 150.

III. BEING AVAILABLE TO GOD
INTRODUCTION

1. Henri J.M. Nouwen, *Making All Things New*, New York: Harper & Row, 1981, p. 90.

2. David Steindl-Rast, *Gratefulness*, Ramsey: Paulist Press, 1984, p. 52.

7. IDOLS, ANXIETIES, AND LETTING GO IN THE DARK

1. Anthony Bloom, *Beginning To Pray*, Ramsey: Paulist Press, 1970, p. xvii.

2. Thomas Merton, "Learning To Live," in *University on the Heights*, ed. W. First, New York: Doubleday and Company, 1969. Text used: for private circulation only, p. 7.

3. Anthony Bloom, *Beginning To Pray*, Ramsey: Paulist Press, 1970, pp. xv, xvi.

4. Karl Rahner, *Encounters with Silence*, Westminster: Newman Press, 1965, p. 5.

5. *Ibid.*

6. Yushi Nomura, *Desert Wisdom*, New York: Doubleday, 1982, p. 26.

7. James Finley, *Merton's Palace of Nowhere*, Notre Dame: Ave Maria, 1978, p. 33.

8. Marian Mill Preminger, *The Sands of Tamanrasset*, New York: Hawthorne, 1961, pp. 95–96.

9. Karl Rahner, *Foundation of Christian Faith*, New York: Seabury, 1978, p. 2.

8. EXPERIENCING THE LORD

1. Urban Holmes III, *Spirituality for Ministry*, New York: Harper & Row, 1982, p. 148.

2. Thomas Merton, *Conjectures of a Guilty Bystander*, New York: Doubleday, 1966, p. 71.

3. J.-P. Dubois-Dumée, "Renewal of Prayer," *Lumen Vitae*, *38*, 3, 1983, pp. 273–274.

4. James Finley, *Merton's Palace of Nowhere*, Notre Dame: Ave Maria, 1978, p. 117.

5. Trevanian, *The Summer of Katya*, New York: Crown, 1983, p. 44.

6. Henri J.M. Nouwen, *The Way of the Heart*, New York: Seabury, 1981, p. 20.

7. Richard Hauser, *In His Spirit*, Ramsey: Paulist Press, 1982, p. 61.

EPILOGUE: IN THE PRESENCE OF GOD

1. Henri J.M. Nouwen, *Clowning in Rome*, New York: Doubleday, 1979, p. 70.

2. Jean Renoir, *Renoir, My Father*, Boston: Little-Brown, 1958, p. 54.

3. Anthony Bloom, *Beginning To Pray*, Ramsey: Paulist, 1970, p. 39.

4. Robert Wicks, *Christian Introspection*, New York: Crossroad, 1983, pp. 13, 100.

5. Kenneth Leech, *True Prayer*, San Francisco: Harper & Row, 1980, p. 36.

6. William Johnston (ed.), *The Cloud of Unknowing*, New York: Doubleday/Image, 1973, p. 101.

7. Bloom, *op. cit.*, pp. 17–18.

About the Author

Dr. Robert Wicks is Director of the Graduate Program in Pastoral Counseling at Neumann College (Aston, PA) and maintains a private practice in Philadelphia. He is a member of the Counseling Committee for Religious of the Archdiocese of Philadelphia, Book Review Editor for the National Association of Catholic Chaplains, General Editor of Integration Books (Paulist Press), and a columnist for the *Catholic Star Herald* (Camden, NJ).

Dr. Wicks is a graduate of Hahnemann Medical College as well as Fairfield and St. John's Universities. He has taught in universities on both the graduate and undergraduate levels, and in professional schools of psychology, theology, medicine, nursing and social work. In addition, he has directed mental health treatment programs in the United States and the Orient.

He has published nineteen books, including *Christian Introspection* (Crossroad) and *Clinical Handbook of Pastoral Counseling* (Paulist).